Becoming and Belonging
SUPPORTING THE HEALTHY SOCIAL-EMOTIONAL DEVELOPMENT OF THE YOUNG CHILD

The WECAN Early Childhood Research Group

Edited by Holly Koteen Soulé

WECAN
WALDORF EARLY CHILDHOOD
ASSOCIATION OF NORTH AMERICA

Becoming and Belonging: Supporting the Healthy Social-Emotional Development of the Young Child

© 2024 Waldorf Early Childhood Association of North America

All rights reserved. No part of this book may be reproduced in any form without the written permission of the publisher, except for brief quotations for the purposes of review.

ISBN: 978-1-936849-61-1

This publication is made possible by a grant from the Waldorf Curriculum Fund.

Cover image © Joanna VonCulin. Used with permission.
Editor: Holly Koteen-Soulé
Assistant Editor: Nancy Blanning

The WECAN Early Childhood Research Group: Nancy Blanning, Laurie Clark, Stephanie Hoelscher, Ruth Ker, Holly Koteen-Soulé, Rihana Rutledge, Rachel Turner, Leslie Wetzonis-Woolverton

Design and Layout: Amy Thesing, amythesing.net

Published in the United States by:

WECAN
WALDORF EARLY CHILDHOOD
ASSOCIATION OF NORTH AMERICA

The Waldorf Early Childhood Association of North America
285 Hungry Hollow Road
Spring Valley, New York 10977

info@waldorfearlychildhood.org
www.waldorfearlychildhood.org
store.waldorfearlychildhood.org

Dedication

To our teachers and mentors who guided us on our path in Waldorf early childhood education: we are so grateful for your generosity!

To our colleagues who support children and families in Waldorf classrooms all over the world: we are heartened by your faithfulness!

To the future teachers who will carry on this work of the heart: we are inspired by your courage!

The WECAN Early Childhood Research Group came together during 2020 with the purpose of sensing how to support our colleagues, children, and families in these turbulent times. It quickly became apparent that our emotional life, especially that of the children, needed attention. This book is a response to the pressing social questions arising in our Waldorf movement and beyond.

NANCY BLANNING, LAURIE CLARK, STEPHANIE HOELSCHER,
RUTH KER, HOLLY KOTEEN-SOULÉ
RIHANA RUTLEDGE, RACHEL TURNER, AND
LESLIE WETZONIS-WOOLVERTON

BECOMING AND BELONGING

Contents

Dedication 3

Editor's Preface 7

Introduction: Why Now? 11

1: The Landscape of Social-Emotional Development
   in the First Seven Years 19
   Holly Koteen Soulé

2: Relationship: Anchor and Sail 29
   Stephanie Hoelscher

3: Beholding the Child 43
   Laurie Clark

4: Sensory Development as the Foundation for a Healthy
   Social-Emotional Life 55
   Nancy Blanning

5: Re-Membering Play 73
   Stephanie Hoelscher

6: The Healing Power of Social Games 99
   Ruth Ker

7: "Here I Am!" Positive Identity Development for Every Child .. 107
   Leslie Wetzonis-Woolverton

8: Face to Face, Heart to Heart, and Full of Imagination! 127
   Holly Koteen-Soulé

9: The Healing Deed 143
   Ruth Ker

10: Soul Nutrition 157
   Rihana Rutledge

11: The Chalice of Community:
   The Social Art of the Waldorf Early Childhood Teacher 171
   Holly Koteen-Soulé

12: Hope: A Tonic for the Future............................... 181
   Laurie Clark

APPENDICES

I. The Essentials of Waldorf Early Childhood Education 197
   Susan Howard

II. The Child Contemplation Form: A Potent Tool for
   Waldorf Schools in Challenging Times 213
   *Laurie Clark, in collaboration with
   the WECAN Early Childhood Research Group*

III. The Sevenfold Path—An Outline for Child Contemplation ... 218
   Laurie Clark

IV. Rudolf Steiner's Six Basic Exercises 223

V. The Artistic Meeting: Creating Space for Spirit 226
   Holly Koteen-Soulé

EDITOR'S PREFACE
Relationship: The I in You and the You in Me

She stood alone. Outside the circle, on the periphery, days into weeks, autumn into winter. She did not eat, not the snack prepared at school nor the lunch brought from home each day in a bright pink case toted by a hurried father rushing to get to work at his new job, in a new place, in a new home, and frantic and on edge at needing to separate from his unhappy child. She did not cry when her father left. She withdrew; she retreated into herself, her body tense and rigid. The sight and touch of her new school's white bunny out in the yard each morning brought moments of solace, visible in the softening of her brow. Unlike noisy classmates or strange masked teachers, this living creature asked nothing of her. Her mother, shocked and distraught by her "social" child's failure to thrive at school, always remembered to tuck a carrot into the pocket of her daughter's jacket. The child clutched the carrot like a talisman until ready to let it go. She prepared a space of inner courage for herself by sitting alone with the rabbit, whispering his name, stroking his fur, and finally feeding him the carrot. Change of any kind shattered this safe space. She ran. She froze. She was afraid.

And so, we start over each day. We know that the most important human skill is learning to be in relationship with others, and that this development comes at a time when outside forces endanger the right of children to be children in the fullest sense of the word. We have learned to recognize the signs of stress in the children's bodies and behavior. As spiritually sensitive beings, children take in the inner disposition of those around them. Attunement to the needs of another is essential for human communication and relationships. Holding reverence for the smallest of moments, allowing time and space for the children to be, and trusting in the mystery wisdom of the children helps us to find the inner attitude of healing that is needed to move forward.

> *Her classmates held a space in the circle for her. "Come fix our crack," they called. "We need you." She stood silent, head bowed and looking downward at the slab of gray granite beneath her feet. Two children walked from the circle to stand alongside her. Warm sun, cool breeze, soundless save for the rustling of leaves. Enfolded into a space of security created by other children, she raised her head and looked out into the world. The three children stood together silently. The other children watched without speaking.*

When we smile, the whole world smiles with us. Children who see positive, radiant faces are more likely to thrive. For several years young children have lived in a world where faces have been masked, and not in predictable or consistent ways. We have done our best to speak with our eyes and to hold an inner warming mood of joy in order to build trust with the children in our care, particularly children new to us. While we have yet to fully understand the impact of masking on the development of young children—social, emotional, and language development—we have witnessed the healing mood brought to the children when the full countenance of the human face is available to them.

> *"Everyone is so happy!" said the children, parents, and teachers upon being liberated from masking. With faces visible, speech clearly articulated, and voices elevated in song, the social world of school underwent nothing less than a*

transformation. Smiles and more smiles. Crinkled noses. All the children played. The little girl played as well, day after day. She chattered like a magpie to her teachers; she clamored for attention; she held her teacher's hand. Her classmates came to appreciate her poet's eye for beauty and her reverence for all living things. And then her family got sick. After a long absence from school, she returned wearing a mask. It was clear that her body carried the burden of it all, but she was able to accept the accompanying presence of her teachers. In the woods she ran up to her teacher. The teacher saw a look of distress approaching panic in the child's eyes. "I can't breathe. I just can't breathe." The teacher paused. "Take it off. Just take it off. It is safe for you." The child looked up at her teacher as she clawed the mask from her face and shoved it in her pocket. She ran off and returned moments later with a flat piece of gray slate. "I used another rock to draw on this rock," she said, as she handed the slate to her teacher. "I love you."

The child had etched the shape of a heart into the piece of gray slate.

Each day, every encounter, one heart at a time. Children, parents, colleagues. Our earnest, heartfelt striving for understanding becomes a healing deed. This asks a lot of us. Parents come as they come.

"I got the time of the picnic wrong," the mother told the teacher in an email. "My daughter was very sad that she missed the last day of school."

In the words of another parent:

"I dug deep to hold onto hope this year, despite so many doubts and lots of fears. What happened this year for my son in terms of his growth has been more and better than anything I might have dreamt in my wildest dreams." This mother gave her son's teacher a drawing that he had done. "He told

me that it is a picture of the two of you. I can't tell who is who, and he won't tell me. Maybe you will know." The two figures are mirror images indistinguishable from each other save for a spiral of red hair. For the teacher it represented "The I in You, the You in Me."

INTRODUCTION:
Why Now?

The spiritual aliveness of the young child is a state of being that many adults spend the rest of their lives trying to find again. Those of us who are privileged to work with children know how precious their wide-open wonder at the world is. Our own souls are softened every day by the silvery drops of their "fresh-as-morning" view.

We also know, only too keenly, how the open-hearted gesture of the young child can go unnoticed or be misunderstood. Despite the growing body of research about a child's critical developmental needs during the early years, the grown-up world doesn't always heed the signposts: "Slow Down," "Less is More," "Pay Attention!" Recent events have actually increased the pressure of outside influences on both children and families.

Covid-19 upended our daily routines and made safety our primary focus for a long time. It also brought fear, uncertainty, and masks into our lives. The feeling of "being safe" took on new meaning during the pandemic. Distancing from friends had an isolating effect and brought "soul stress" to the children. Teachers responded creatively by moving most of their classrooms outdoors and rediscovering the essential elements of Waldorf early childhood education. While the resulting accommodations were positive, it became clear, nonetheless, that having to cope with an ever-changing situation took its toll, not only on the children, but also on families and teachers.

BECOMING AND BELONGING

The reawakened social justice movement brought much needed attention to untransformed areas of our shared social life and our Waldorf movement, as well. Making any real progress in our commitment to diversity, equity, and inclusion requires honest self-evaluation and sincere, sustained efforts. Even though there has been some hopeful momentum, this is a task that we cannot put down. Continued progress will require our ongoing attention.

Both of these issues have divided individuals and groups into ideologically opposed camps with little will to engage in civil discourse. This polarization has grown to include additional hot-button social issues, such as abortion, LGBTQ rights, climate change, and cultural appropriation vs. cultural appreciation.

The recognition of the impacts of these issues on the social-emotional life of the young child prompted the WECAN Early Childhood Research Group to re-examine the essential aspects of Waldorf early childhood education. How can early childhood educators better support children to meet our current social challenges? How can we prepare them to meet the social challenges of the future?

The first Waldorf school began in the chaotic social aftermath of World War I with a clear social mission. At the heart of Waldorf Education was the hope that by cultivating independent thinking, compassion for others, and moral courage, the next generation could bring healing impulses to the many social problems of the early 1900s. There are now Waldorf schools in over sixty different countries. While the circumstances in each country vary, the need for social healing is as great as ever.

In this collection of articles, we look at the principles and practices of Waldorf early childhood education in the light of the need for social and emotional healing. We want to inspire authentic enthusiasm in ourselves for life that allows all children to feel a sense of trust and safety in our Waldorf communities. We want to help children develop a deep reservoir of resilience in these tumultuous times. We want to cultivate faith in the goodness of humanity that will allow us all to meet the future with the courage of our convictions.

CHAPTER SUMMARIES

1: The Landscape of Social-Emotional Development in the First Seven Years

In this chapter we survey specific aspects of the processes of becoming and belonging for the young child. We look at the importance of the primary relationship between the baby and the parent or caregiver and the significant influences of family and cultural life on the child's growing social-emotional capacities. We explore the role of empathy in our social-emotional development and in our culture. How do the principles of Waldorf early childhood education support the social-emotional needs of the young child and offer healing impulses to the larger social world that we all live in and create together?

2: Relationship: Anchor and Sail

In this chapter we focus on the central role of relationships in social life. We look at the qualities of relationships that can nurture every child's growing social capacities. How can we become more present, attentive, attuned, and responsive? As we strive to fulfill our intention to nurture the young child, what matters is that we are steadfast in our relationships with parents and colleagues, as well as with the children in our care. Each of us weaves and is woven into a dynamic and complex web of relationships that affects the well-being of the children in our care. Conscious engagement in understanding what constitutes social health supports us all.

3: Beholding the Child

In this chapter we illuminate the uniqueness of Waldorf pedagogy in that it is not a prescribed methodology, but rather a living process. We practice child observation with a general understanding of child development in view, but without standardized goals and measurements for individual children. We acknowledge the spiritual developmental wisdom that lives in the child and accompanies the child's creative unfolding.

4: Sensory Development as the Foundation for a Healthy Social-Emotional Life

In this chapter, the importance of healthy development of the twelve senses, as described by Rudolf Steiner, is explored in multiple ways. Each child spends the years from birth to seven developing an experience of security, shelter, and comfort in the physical body through the four foundational senses of touch, life sense/well-being, self-movement, and balance. In a truly literal way, the health of each of these sensory systems lays the foundation for individual emotional health and a harmonious social life. Understanding this foundation, our awareness of the importance of the work we do with children through touch, movement, rhythm and routine, challenging physical play, and sequential practical work greatly expands. Learning to read the signs of healthy or distressed senses opens up new doors to understanding challenging behaviors we see with children in our care.

5: Re-Membering Play

In this chapter we look at how we can restore the healing power of play to children. Play flows like a river, subterranean at times, bursting forth to reveal a child's inner drive to make meaning and mirth in their world. Play is the purest expression of what it means to be a child. Waldorf educators have been long-standing advocates for play. Our classrooms are not play-deprived. While it is now even more apparent how critical play is for a child's mental health and well-being, it also is apparent that teachers need to think openly about their role in facilitating play for children. This chapter considers how we might remove the blockages and let the river of play flow freely, into a wider sustaining stream of life for the children in our care. What does it mean to facilitate play? How do environmental spaces and materials affect our creative thinking? How do adult perceptions of risk influence children's experiences of play? What can be amplified to help children return to the joyful flow of creative and imaginative play? Finally, how does our own playfulness figure into this?

6: The Healing Power of Social Games

In this chapter we explore how playing games in the early childhood classroom supports children in developing social skills. It also helps children playfully release stress and build healthy social habits. Introducing a variety of original games, traditional games, fingerplays, and songs from around the world can help harmonize the social atmosphere of the whole class and also have healing effects for the individual child.

7: "Here I am!" Positive Identity Development for Every Child

In this chapter we examine more deeply how a child forms a positive sense of self that includes the child's racial, ethnic, cultural, and gender identity. This self-identification process begins early, even before the baby's first steps. We need to understand how the school environment and the actions of teachers and caregivers significantly affect a child's emerging sense of self. How can we affirm the dignity of each child and their contribution to the class? Consciously taking up antibias work is an essential aspect of social-emotional health in our classrooms and school communities. The work of being together is heart work, a task of the highest order. It serves each of us and builds up the community that can hold us all, even in trying times.

8: Face to Face, Heart to Heart, and Full of Imagination! Speech as the Living Bridge between the Emerging Self and the World

In this chapter we explore language acquisition and how it is connected to social development. Children acquire language through imitation. They hunger for opportunities to experience the warmth and expressive qualities of face-to-face conversations. Supporting a child's growing ability to communicate begins with paying attention and responding to a child's nonverbal cues. The child's language development goes through several stages from concrete to imaginative pictures to the dawn of abstract thinking. Children respond best to simple living pictures rather than lengthy intellectual explanations. Pauses allow children time to digest what has been said and to respond, and also the opportunity to become comfortable with silence. The capacity to listen to a child with true interest builds confidence and trust in the child. Another way that a child learns to trust is when the adult is true to their word.

9: The Healing Deed

In this chapter we look at the impact that early childhood teachers can have as healers. An understanding word or an empathetic deed can have a profound effect on children who are struggling. Sensing into a child's state of being and supportively accompanying the child can be life-affirming and life-strengthening. Healing moments can arise every day in the early childhood classroom. When educators are attentive to those moments, they can make a difference in the lives of children and their families.

10: Soul Nutrition

In this chapter we focus on our own health and healing. Our path of inner development may include finding ways to reduce the stresses of our current situation and to replenish our forces. Biographical exercises and artistic activities are both rejuvenating. These activities and our inner exercises can also support our antibias work. A teacher, parent, or caregiver needs to fill the well so that thirsty children have water to drink.

11: The Chalice of Community: The Social Art of the Waldorf Early Childhood Teacher

In this chapter we look at the ever-evolving community-building work with our children, their families, and our school communities. We wish to cultivate a sense of collaboration in all of these groups. We want to expand our cultural awareness to enrich the experiences of children and families. How can we listen with new openness and work together as co-researchers on questions of mutual interest? Our work includes acknowledging and honoring the mutuality that binds us together in this place and time on behalf of the children.

12: Hope: A Tonic for the Future

This chapter is a testament to our joy in the work and our hope for the future of the children. Hope for the future calls us to actively cherish one another and create a sacred space around the children. This space requires honesty, transparency, authenticity, and respect for the autonomy of others. Cooperation beyond the limits of language, politics, and religion is possible when we are aspiring to create "The Beloved Community." This work calls for persistent determination and willingness to stretch and widen the heart. The truth of love elevates us all and offers a vision of the world where everyone thrives.

BECOMING AND BELONGING

1:
The Landscape of Social-Emotional Development in the First Seven Years

Holly Koteen Soulé

It is spring and a grandmother is pruning the raspberries with her three-year-old granddaughter. They are taking turns with the shears.

The little girl stops, looks up, and speaks with great seriousness. "Look up there, Baba. Do you see that?" The grandmother looks up as the girl continues. "When I see that love-and-light, I just go like this."

She motions with both hands, forming two side-by-side ovals in the air. Then her right hand goes to her mouth and she says, "It comes right in here and goes down to my tummy." She places both hands on her belly. "And then I give it out to everyone in the world." She extends both hands out in front of her.

Then she goes back to the task at hand.

What are the lingering effects of the Covid pandemic and other recent social disruptions in our communities? What are the children asking of us? How can we best respond? These are some of the questions we are asking ourselves. More and more, it seems as if the answers need to be lived and experienced. In many instances, the answers may be unique to an individual child or to a particular community. What is becoming increasingly clear is that the questions we are asking will help us deepen our understanding of our work, our changing world, and the children in our care. The following topics are signposts for us as we survey the current landscape to find ways to support the young child's development.

Becoming and Belonging

Becoming and belonging are two life processes in which every human being participates. They are polar processes: in becoming, we move inwardly toward ourselves, and in belonging, we move outwardly toward others. They are also complementary because whatever happens in one informs the other. However, human beings are not closed systems. We exist in a mutuality with our surroundings and our communities. Our biographies, both individual and collective, weave us together, often in mysterious ways. Our social-emotional life flows and grows between us.

In Waldorf education we refer to the process of becoming in the first twenty-one years as *incarnation*, meaning we take hold of our lives in the first three seven-year phases of development. From birth to seven years of age, the child primarily takes hold of the physical body. During this time, however, the seeds of future social-emotional, intellectual, and spiritual capacities are also being nurtured and, if well-rooted, will bear fruit in later developmental periods.

In the first seven years, these future capacities, including the social-emotional capacities, are nested within the child's physical development. Prior to the birth of the child's own etheric body, the child's surroundings, and especially the adult human beings close to the child, form a kind of womb in which foundational patterns for the child's future relationships are embedded. What the child experiences as organic resonances with its surroundings live in the child's psychosomatic heritage of the first seven years.

Chapter 1: The Landscape of Social-Emotional Development in the First Seven Years

After the birth of the child's own etheric body, at around the age of seven, children achieve a separateness from their surroundings that now allows them to begin to have a conscious awareness of the difference between their experiences in the outer world and their own inner experiences. During the period from seven to fourteen years of age, what we typically define as the feeling life, or the social-emotional life, really begins. What has taken place during the first seven years, however, has been deeply integrated into the child's body and soul and will significantly influence continued development in the social-emotional realm.

Reciprocity: A Cornerstone of Social-Emotional Development

A newborn baby orients itself toward the parent or caregiver like a planet to the sun. Dr. Bessel Van Der Kolk, in his book *The Body Keeps the Score*, explains what scientists believe to be the physiological basis for the way in which the baby attunes to the caregiver and vice versa. The discovery in 1994 of specialized cells in the cortex of the brain, called mirror neurons, explained many previously unexplained aspects of the human mind, such as empathy, imitation, synchrony, and even language acquisition. Through the activity of the mirror neurons, the baby picks up on the movements, emotional states and intentions of the caregiver.[1]

Dr. Van Der Kolk emphasizes that, "Social support is not the same as merely being in the presence of others. The critical issue is reciprocity: being truly heard and seen by other people around us, feeling we are held in someone else's mind and heart. For our physiology to calm down, heal and grow, we need a visceral feeling of safety."[2] Through the caregiver's sensitive attunement and responsiveness to the child, a secure relationship begins to be formed.

With the sensitive attunement and support of the caregiver, young children also begin to sense the difference between situations they can manage and situations where they need help. This is the foundation of learning how to self-regulate, self-soothe, and self-nurture. Young human beings learn how to care for themselves and ultimately how to care for others based on how they are cared for. Research cited by Dr. Van Der Kolk also indicates that resilience, or a child's capacity to bounce back from adversity, is predicted by the level of security established with the primary caregiver in the first two years of life.[3]

Because of young children's openness to their surroundings, they are deeply affected by everything they experience, but especially by the human beings around them and the quality of their social interactions. Indirectly, children are also affected by the social atmosphere in which their caretakers are embedded. What is clearly true for the very young child also applies to older children and adolescents in different but no less impactful ways. The obvious effects of Covid-19 on children's lives is an example that we all have witnessed.

We Live in Stressful Times

Given what we know about the openness and vulnerability of young children to their surroundings, it is easy to understand how overwhelming events or ongoing adverse circumstances can cause trauma for young children and negatively impact their health and development. What is becoming increasingly clear in recent years is that the cumulative effect of small everyday stresses can also be detrimental. These everyday stresses may include erratic attention from parents and caregivers, excessive exposure to media, lack of rhythm, and insufficient unscheduled time. Too much intellectual stimulation and not enough engagement in sensory and imaginative activities can also contribute to a child's daily stress.

According to Dr. Gabor Maté, these everyday stresses on children may be traced to the environmental pressures placed on all of us by certain attributes of our modern society. In other words, when parents are stressed, children will be stressed. While economic insecurity, systemic racism, unsafe living conditions, and insufficient access to health care or education are the more obvious social factors that induce stress and stress-related behaviors, Dr. Maté, in his book *The Myth of Normal*, describes additional equally pervasive social factors that work against healthy family life:

> Our cultural ecology does not support attuned, present, responsive, connected parenting. As we have seen, the destabilization begins with stress transmitted to infants still in the womb, with the mechanization of birth, the attenuation of parenting instinct, the denial of the child's developmental needs. It continues with the increasingly intolerable economic and social pressures on parents these days and the erosion of communities, and magnifies the disinformation that parents receive on how to rear their young. Reinforced by the educational systems that too often stress students with pressures to compete, the process culminates in the exploitation of children and youth for the glory of the consumer market.[4]

A common significant symptom of stress is disconnection. Temporarily disconnecting from physical or emotional stress allows an individual to cope with what is happening in the moment. In situations of chronic stress, however, we are at risk of habitually disconnecting from ourselves, from one another, and from meaningful activity in the world. Our society's emphasis on individualism, competition, and material achievement rather than community, collaboration, and creativity is moving us unconsciously toward a possible future of increasing alienation and loneliness. Disconnection impacts our mental and physical health.

For Dr. Maté, the good news is that becoming aware of these environmental pressures can empower us to advocate for the kind of changes that we know will support individual and social healing and health. He is encouraged by recent research that acknowledges the intrinsic relationship of mind and body, recognizes the impact of our relationships on our health and well-being, and promotes the understanding of disease as less of a "thing" and more of a process.

BECOMING AND BELONGING

Empathy Matters

Bruce Perry and Maia Szalavitz, in their book *Born for Love*, explore human relationships in the light of empathy. They explain that while we are all born to nurture and be nurtured, our natural sense of empathy, like so many other biological gifts, requires specific experiences to develop. In the young child, empathy, or feeling with what others feel, is at first an innate set of unconscious responses without the child's being able to distinguish between self and others.

When empathy is reciprocated, first by the primary caregiver and later by others, it becomes rooted firmly in the soul and begins to grow.

Empathy and stress are intimately connected. When a child feels emotionally secure, the child is able to manage the small doses of stress that come with experiencing new situations. The authors explain that a little stress keeps both children and adults alert, while stress that is too intense or too long-lasting brings on fear and compromises our potential for learning.[5]

Perry and Szalavitz draw attention to the challenging reality, noting that while our human need for social contact is no less essential than ever, we are living in a time of relational poverty. Meaningful relationships are in decline and our social fabric is disintegrating. In their view, this puts the development of empathy at risk. "Empathy allows us to relieve one another's stress and .... It is central to human joy. And we need more of it than ever before to deal with the complex challenges created by our rapidly changing institutions, diverse communities and distressed planet."[6]

Through empathy we learn to connect with another human being. Through empathy we learn how to respond to new situations and manage physical and emotional stress. Through empathy we learn how to relate to different kinds of people. Developing empathy requires practice. How can we support rich social environments in our Waldorf classrooms that allow empathy to grow and flourish in ourselves and in the children?

Chapter 1: The Landscape of Social-Emotional Development in the First Seven Years

Creating a Space for Emotional Well-Being

Although there were no Waldorf Kindergartens established before his death, Rudolf Steiner spoke extensively about the nature of the young child. A central theme was the idea of imitation as the primary means by which the young child takes in and learns about the world. This idea has, of course, been subsequently confirmed by child development researchers. The importance of imitation requires that we early childhood educators work hard to be worthy of imitation. This principle, and the commitment it requires to self-improvement, is one of several principles that continue to inform our work.[7]

Reverence, repetition, and rhythm is an alliterative phrase often used to describe certain aspects of Waldorf early childhood education. In thinking about our topic of social-emotional health and development, those three words take on a fuller, richer meaning.

Reverence has to do not only with the mood of devotion to our everyday tasks, but also to the way in which we view a child. Reverence for the child means that we see each child as a unique being with particular gifts. Can we be faithful to this view even when a child brings us mysterious challenges? Can we accept the child with an open heart and mind, be curious about the child's behaviors, and have a real interest in creating space for the child and family in our class? If we can, then the child will feel affirmed in their emerging sense of self.

Repetition implies constancy and consistency. One of the most important factors in supporting children who have experienced trauma or stress is a consistent adult figure who is willing to be fully present for them. When children's trust has to be rebuilt, they will test us again and again until they see that we are dependable. In a way, their trust reflects our trust in their process of healing. When a teacher models a consistent belief in a child's capacity for social-emotional healing, then it helps the other children in the class to do the same.

Rhythm is how we order time and space. A predictable rhythm gives young children, who do not yet have a relationship to clock time, a sense of security. That everything has a specific place in the classroom is equally comforting. A more subtle aspect of working with rhythm is the breathing between child-directed and teacher-guided activities. Do we orchestrate this breathing in a regimented manner, or can we sense and adjust it to meet the needs of the group or individual children? An even more subtle aspect of working with rhythm takes place when a teacher senses the need to provide emotional stability for a child who has become emotionally overwhelmed.

Creating a Space for Social Healing

Play is the work of a child and Waldorf early childhood education has always championed the importance of play for the child's healthy development. In the context of the child's social-emotional life, play serves as a readily available way to digest and work through challenging experiences. It also brings children into safe social contact and new relationships. More often than not, creative play is a shared social activity that also builds a sense of community within the class.

The commitment of Waldorf schools to diversity and inclusion has increased our awareness of the importance of belonging, not only for individual children, but also to the families who comprise our Waldorf communities. We need to look at how we can be more inclusive in our outreach, enrollment, and interview processes and in how we can be more welcoming of diversity in our community building. The ever-present need for social healing exists both within and beyond our school communities.

In the lectures that Rudolf Steiner gave to the teachers of the first Waldorf School, he spoke about what he saw as the essential mood surrounding the young child. In the first seven years, he said, a child has the unconscious assumption that *the world is good*.[8] How can *goodness* be a daily living reality in our classrooms? This does not mean everything will be perfect, not at all! It means that we will carry on, with the knowledge that we are all in this healing work together and that we carry hope in one pocket and trust in the other.

Chapter 1: The Landscape of Social-Emotional Development in the First Seven Years

ADDITIONAL RESOURCES:

Dögl, P., E. M. Rishke, and U. Strub. *Beginning Well*. Spring Valley, NY: Waldorf Early Childhood Association of North America, 2018.

Long-Breipohl. R.. *Under the Stars: The Foundations of Steiner Waldorf Early Childhood Education*. Gloucestershire, UK: Hawthorn Press, 2012.

ENDNOTES

1. B. Van Der Kolk, *The Body Keeps the Score: Brain, Mind, and Body in the Healing of Trauma* (New York: Penguin Books, 2014), 58.
2. Ibid, 81.
3. Ibid, 163.
4. G. Maté, *The Myth of Normal: Trauma, Illness, and Healing in a Toxic Culture* (New York: Penguin Random House, 2022), 180.
5. M. Szalavitz and B. Perry, *Born for Love: Why Empathy Is Essential—And Endangered* (New York: Mariner Books, 2011), 311.
6. Ibid, 308.
7. Susan Howard, in "The Essentials of Waldorf Early Childhood Education," appendix I in this volume, extrapolates the key principles from Steiner's lectures.
8. R. Steiner, *The Foundations of Human Experience* (Hudson, NY: Anthroposophic Press, 1996), 158.

BECOMING AND BELONGING

2:
Relationship: Anchor and Sail
Stephanie Hoelscher

All flourishing is mutual.

—ROBIN WALL KIMMERER

A father folded his lanky, angular frame into the straight-backed wooden chair. His daughter's chair. Shifting his weight onto his knees, he leaned forward as his gaze took in the surroundings of what was his child's first school home. He smiled broadly as I, the teacher, told him of his daughter's trust and courage in adapting not just to the space of school but to a place where language, environment, food, and culture were not what she knew. With some bemusement he told me how his daughter now corrected his English at home.

He leaned in closer with a direct gaze before continuing, "My wife and I talk about this, about what my daughter is learning here at school. We see that she is learning to be a good person. Nothing is more important to us than this, to be a good person."

Introduction

A child enters the world. First breath. The breath of life: *Re-spir-ation.*

My breath, my body, my people, my place.

BECOMING AND BELONGING

I breathe on my own. My basic biologic process is autonomic and unconscious. Everything else about my being and its development is affected by the world around me. Some of this I will see and experience directly. Most I will experience through others.

Experiences will build my brain, but my brain does not live alone. It lives in connection with the rest of my body, and this is critically important for my development. Relationships—the nested circles of interwoven realities from stars to planets, from mountains to rivers, from humans to more humans—will build me, and so I need you.

I need people who care, whom I can count on, who see me and love me for who I am and who I am meant to become. I hear in the breath of my people that they need the same. They too need others who care and appreciate them for all the ways in which they are different from each other, even with all our human imperfections. As different as we are from one another, as unique as each one of us is, we are much more the same than we are different. That is a very important message to impart to us children. It will help us grow toward being caring, compassionate, and charitable adults.

Some of you will become my teachers. Teachers, dear teachers, you will need my family. Family, dear family, you will need my teachers. I need you to be curious and interested in each other. We are complicated and fascinating creatures, you know, with such stories to share. Each of us has a light to bring to the other. To give and receive each other's light is a gift for the world. How I hope that you will treat each other with tenderness and respect. A very wise person poetically urged us to have "soft eyes" with each other. Is that not a beautiful image to guide us in our everyday interactions with each other! Too much is at stake here; the task too arduous for us not to recognize that the spaces in between us are calling out for connection. We need to do this together anew and always renewing.

I may come to you as more of a mystery than you were expecting. Please reach deep within yourself to be patient with what you do not understand. I have wisdom, as do you. Please listen to the echoes of our shared inner wisdom. It will help to guide you in how and what you teach me about the world. It will be many years before I will be ready to walk alone without you close by.

The earth also needs people who care, and I can hear the earth's loneliness in its broadest and most intimate of spaces. Please listen. I need you to listen deeply. Listening is where love begins: listening to ourselves, to each other, to our natural and social worlds.

Some of what is most important for you to hear—and important as a bridge for understanding and connection—will not come to you from what I say in words. My body will speak to you. It will tell you when I am afraid. My eyes will speak to you. They will tell you when I feel safe and protected—or not. Understanding how my body holds emotions and experiences will help me learn how to find my balance. I will need your help with this as well. When I feel that the earth is firm beneath my feet, I become a tree with roots deep and branches strong, a sanctuary for myself and for others.

Please be attentive. I need your true attention so that I may feel safe. The world is going too fast for me, and I need you to notice your own habits, pace, practices, and inclinations. Presence is more important than productivity. This is something I need to learn from you. I need to see stillness in you, so that I may learn that as well. When you have inner stillness and are attentive and slow down, you will experience remarkable delights in life along with me, things like the furry caterpillar that unfurls from his tight ball to stretch and creep across the path in the late morning sun. How special it could be for us to have time to linger over such discoveries together. I bet you can feel in your body what it was like to watch bees in your grandmother's flower garden. Does this memory not bring a smile to your face? Please remember these "little joys"; they are the slender threads of which we weave the lifeline that connects us to a world beyond ourselves. I want to say yes to life, even though I may sometimes see the shadow side of the human condition. Please help me to be confident as I enter into my earthly life.

BECOMING AND BELONGING

Finally, I must say that many of you need to learn to breathe again. I need you to show me how to breathe beautifully, to breathe truly and deeply. We cannot breathe well without each other. I cannot breathe well without you, and do you know what happens in the rhythms of our shared re-spir-ation? We take in a breath that is connected to a healing spirit.

> *Our belonging is rooted in the living body of the Earth, woven of the flows of time and relationship that form our bodies, our communities, our climate.*
>
> —JOANNA MACY

The world around us, the world our children are entering, is hurting. Children face an uncertain future. A joint commission report by the World Health Organization, UNICEF, and the Lancet "finds that climate change, ecological degradation, migrating populations, prolonged and growing conflict, rise in digital technology, pervasive inequalities, and predatory commercial practices threaten the health and future of children in every country."[1] Childhood is protected under the UN Convention on the Rights of the Child. According to the convention, childhood lasts until a person is eighteen years old and is a special, protected time in which children must be allowed to grow, learn, play, develop, and flourish with dignity. But for all the reasons named above, childhood is changing.

> *A high-pitched sound cut through the misty morning as the kindergarten children played. I heard anguish in the sound and walked to where a boy lay thrashing on the wet ground. He pounded the earth with closed fists; he kicked the earth with his sturdy rubber boots. He screamed and he cried, with tears streaking his flushed cheeks and sweat glistening in beads along his hairline.*
>
> *I stood nearby. Close enough but not too close. I saw his eyes move to take in my presence. He knew I was there. Other*

children, curious and caring, came to stand with me. We were silent. The crying and screaming began to ease; the force of the kicking and pounding dissipated.

I saw the child begin to breathe more deeply again. Still lying face down, his chest rose and fell more rhythmically. I took a step closer and paused to see if he was ready. He looked up from the ground, gazed into my eyes and said, "They were looking at me. They were looking at me."

Gaze and Encounter as Anchors

Look at me. Don't look at me. Are you my friend? Can I really trust you?

The gaze is one of the most important cues for human communication and social interaction. The gaze of an infant, which begins at around three months, is open, earnest, and penetrating. An infant does not turn his gaze away. When the steadfast gaze of an infant is returned, the child finds its first stable relationship. The child develops trust in another and participates in the earliest forms of call and response, serve and return, the giving-receiving gift of the divine. These interactive exchanges reveal dialogue in its truest form. Confidence and joy in being part of this world are affirmed in theis encounter.

> *Our task and an anchoring practice is to bring recognition to the power of the loving gaze. To become once again so capable of relating to others as we ourselves were as young child—in order not to disappoint this gaze. Relating begins with seeing and discerning for ourselves how we lift our gaze out into the world.*
>
> —MICHAELA GLÖCKLER

Knowing how to lift the gaze and to respond to another's emotional and physical needs is what it means to *co-regulate*. Co-regulation begins before birth as a baby hears the sounds of its mother's voice. The human voice, the mother's voice, brings comfort.

Mystery and science come together in considering the creative power of human encounter when carried through a loving, wondering, caring gaze. A growing body of research suggests that in face-to-face interactions, the nervous systems of two or more individuals interact in a way that supports mutual well-being and emotional connection.[2] When people co-regulate, their heart rate, respiration, and emotional states can become synchronized. This synchronization often occurs through nonverbal cues, such as facial expression, tone of voice, and touch. In other words, my embodied state communicates safety to you—or not.

Co-regulation, to me, is like keeping good company. In its linguistic roots, to keep company means to share bread with another. In practice—as my best teachers, the children, have taught me—co-regulation means to be present, available, and to respond to someone in need so that the other does not feel alone. There is no single way to keep good company when another is stressed or distressed; fearing, fighting, or frozen; hungry for food, rest, warmth of caring connection. To speak—or not? To touch—or not? To look toward or away? To answer these questions, and more, requires that we pause, slow down, look, and listen. Look and listen again from a place of stillness and wonder. There is no template for co-regulation. It all depends upon this moment with this child in this context and this situation. We must attune to the individual child. When teachers co-regulate or attune their responses to the diverse needs of individual children, they support the skill of self-regulation in a group setting.[3] *Co-regulation depends upon the caregiver's own capacity for self-regulation.*

If we were to identify anchoring practices, I would say that it always comes back to getting closer to the children through our observations and contemplations, to be conscious of our own emotional state and inner mood, and to embrace the mystery of each encounter as a sustaining force. This fosters mutual development. "Without encounter," Dr. Glöckler writes, "there is no development. Development is a creative process of the space between human beings and things—that is why education, if it wants to promote healthy development, is really the forming of relational spaces."[4]

Our inner attitude is an intractable anchor available to help us sail through storms that are often (always!) storms of our own making. Haim Ginott is helpful here: "It is my daily mood that makes the weather. It is my response that decides whether a crisis is escalated or de-escalated, and a person is humanized or dehumanized."[5]

Elevating Routines into Rituals

This is a wonderful day.
I've never seen this one before.

—MAYA ANGELOU

Teacher, you know the bestest part of my day? It is when we do the running line, and I get to whisper what animal I am into your ear and then I get to run as hard and fast as I can down the hill unless it's one of those days when I roll down the hill because I am a roly-poly or I hop down the hill because I am a frog or I crawl down the hill because I am a kitty. Or, you know Teacher, some days I just want to wait. Just wait and not do any of that stuff. Just wait and walk down together with you.

Actually, the bestest part of my day is when we sit all together and make bread and I smell the bread baking, and I can't wait to eat the bread, and we sing the bread song, and we talk about everything and everyone who helps us be able to make our bread. When I get home after bread day at school, I like telling my big sister that we eat dirt when we eat bread. She says that's yucky. I tell her she's wrong; bread comes from the earth and it's yummy. Yes, that is what I like best.

No, no, no. That's not right. The bestest part of my day is when you wash my hands and face with that warm cloth

> *that smells so good. Oh, I like that. Even when I think I don't want that, I like that. And, teacher, I get all quiet inside when you wash my hands. I know that you know the color of my eyes. That makes me feel good.*

When I think about how a simple act transforms from an unthinking routine to a meaningful ritual, I return to a tea shop that I once stumbled into from outside streets that were so loud and lively they brought me to the edge of overwhelm. It was summer, but I felt cold. I had a map crammed into my pocket, but I felt lost. Those feelings evaporated when I entered this space that was entirely unremarkable in its material furnishings. Among long benches next to long tables where fragments of conversations flowed quietly between and among those drinking tea, the tea shop lady silently floated about filling cups and wiping tables. It wasn't just that she was all-knowing of of the needsof her patrons—which she was. Nor was it just that her inner stillness suffused the space with a calm time out of time—which she did. It was that the way that everything flowed together, from how she poured the water and wiped the tables to how she gazed in such a manner that strangers all felt they had come home in this moment home. No thoughtful gesture is too small to bring us together.

> *All bread must be broken*
> *so it can be shared. Together*
> *we eat this earth.*
>
> —MARGARET ATWOOD

In this fragment from the poem "All Bread," the poet asks us to pay attention to one small thing, a loaf of bread, and to see all of the things that are gathered within that small thing.[6] This is the revelation, as I see it, of how a weekly "activity," such as the making, baking, and breaking of bread, potentially holds the power of a ritual. The aroma of bread baking in the oven touches the primordial place where human beings are their truest selves.[7] I continue to contemplate the practice of what Orland Bishop calls "sacred hospitality," and I see that practice in the small, simple acts that anchor our social worlds, potentially, in mystery and meaning, caring and connecting that goes beyond the everyday. Bread-making can be more than making bread.

Gestures of caring also offer opportunities for elevating the everyday into a deeper realm of meaning. By *gesture* I mean the expression of a quality that goes beyond the immediate sense-perceptible effect of the action. A caring gesture reaches out to touch body, soul, and spirit.[8] The next time you are washing the hands of a young child, try asking yourself, "What is the truth of water?" What rises up for you internally? Share your insights face-to-face with someone else like a colleague or parent. This is one way we might empower our everyday routines with ritual significance that brings meaning, purpose, and social well-being to self and other(s). Bringing ritual to our everyday actions helps keep us anchored to the higher meaning of our work. Dr. Glöckler expresses this beautifully:

> When we become conscious of what we are doing when washing an infant or toddler, when we are true and honest and let the truth of water live in us, then we wash the child in angel-substance. Then s/he can physically experience what the Guardian angel is spiritually: purity, gentleness, transparency, clarity, cleanliness, morality, regeneration, healing, comfort, refreshment.[9]

Why, I wonder, do we call hand washing a routine? We return to mystery as an anchor. All flourishing is mutual.

Listening Circles: Opening Up Spaces for Encounter

> *We need you to be so curious about each other, dear Big People, and to help each other pause, reflect, and hear the wisdom of your own inner voices. You need special spaces to do this important work. Only when you quiet the chatter of worlds inside and out , when each person is free to be, when you listen—truly listen—can you meet each other. And then,*

> *oh! Once you take up this responsibility, which is every Big Person's responsibility if we are to be in harmony and understanding with each other and nature, the magic of human communication can dance freely. What is then possible? You can create something new together by stepping into this wonderful unknown.*

"Where does your light come from, Teacher?" In our adult circles, how can we help each other find our light and keep it glowing with spirit? As we find ourselves midstream in a paradigm shift within which adults need to concern themselves with questions of self-development and self-reflection,[10] there is a great need for social "homes" that support the unique inner development of adults. What do our circles need in order to foster the freedom, the development, and the greater truth of the other? The social home would be a place of mutual reciprocity and responsibility that recognizes the "I" of the other. A place that follows the principle of Ubuntu, the African wisdom that says, "I am because you are." This may help us weave a fabric of *mutual knowing* that is resilient in the face of issues that otherwise might rip such fabric apart.

What I will call *listening circles* are possible if there is a practice of creating intentional dedicated spaces using a clear process.[11] We need to make places that are safe for the soul to facilitate the inner learning each of us has to do. First, this requires participation in the space to be truly invitational—the individual's choice. Nobody "has to." For example, the common practice of going around a circle for introductions or check-ins at a faculty or parent meeting goes largely unexamined in my experience and looks more like compulsion than invitation. Instead, a facilitator might open a meeting by offering introductions, or any group prompt, as an opportunity to "know and be known," as the individual chooses.[12]

A listening circle is also a calm place where the undivided self can develop and find respect, warmth, and authenticity. The Center for Courage and Renewal, directed by Parker Palmer, uses an

Chapter 2: Relationship: Anchor and Sail

inquiry-based process to create such a space. To be inquiry-based requires a shared commitment to not fixing, advising, "saving," or correcting one another. This asks us to learn to listen deeply and ask questions that help others hear their own inner wisdom more clearly. These questions are not advice in disguise. They have no purpose other than to help someone listen to their inner teacher. In the process everyone learns and grows. Over decades of working with individuals and groups from a diverse range of backgrounds on this inquiry-based process for meeting circles, Palmer has found that people learn to be present in a different way that transforms relationships when fixing or solving is not the purpose. Through the truth-telling of the individual, the group grows closer, while at the same time, the individual finds inner guidance.

To accompany the children in our care in these times asks us to dig deeper into our own development. We can anchor ourselves to the mystery of the gaze and the encounter, use our creativity to make spaces that resonate with the places we live and the people around us, and create places for listening and inner work. These tangible practices will help bring the social forms we need for mutual flourishing, so we can both be anchored and sail forward. It is important, wrote the poet William Stafford, that awake people be awake. Creativity is our human gift. Our world needs us to be awake and awakening to new ways for beholding each other, for the darkness around us is deep. We can use our creativity to support this awakening.

> The first epigraph is from *Braiding Sweetgrass* by Robin Wall Kimmerer. The second is from *A Wild Love for the World: Joanna Macy and the Work of Our Time*, edited by Stephanie Kaza. The third epigraph is from *The Dignity of the Young Child* by Michaela Glöckler and Claudia Grah-Wittich. The third is from @DrMayaAngelou, the author's official Twitter account, May 17, 2013. The fourth is from *Two-Headed Poems* by Margaret Atwood.

REFERENCES

Atwood, Margaret. "All Bread." In *Two-Headed Poems*. New York: Simon & Schuster, 1980.

Bodrova, E. and Leong, D. J. (2006). "Self-Regulation as a Key to School Readiness: How Early Childhood Teachers Can Promote this Critical Competency." In *Critical Issues in Early Childhood Professional Development*, edited by M. Zaslow and I. Martinez-Beck, 203–224. Baltimore, MD: Paul H. Brookes Publishing Co., 2006.

Bohm, David, and Lee Nichol. *On Dialogue*. London: Routledge, 2004.

Buber, Martin. *I and Thou*. Translated by Ronald Gregor Smith. 2nd edition. New York: Charles Scribner's Sons, 1958.

Dana, Deb. *Anchored: How to Befriend Your Nervous System Using Polyvagal Theory*. Boulder, CO: Sounds True, 2021.

Esquirol, Josep Maria. *The Intimate Resistance: A Philosophy of Proximity*. Translated by Douglas Suttle. London: Fum D'Estampa Press, 2015.

Gillespie, Linda Groves. "Rocking and Rolling–It Takes Two: The Role of Co-Regulation in Building Self-Regulation Skills." *Young Children* 70, no. 3 (July 2015). https://www.naeyc.org/resources/pubs/yc/jul2015/rocking-rolling.

Glöckler, Michaela and Claudia Grah-Wittich, eds. *The Dignity of the Young Child*. Dornach, Switzerland: Verlag am Goetheanum, 2019.

Gruwez, Christine. "The Courage to Be a Fragment." *Das Goetheanum*, September 1, 2023. https://dasgoetheanum.com/en/the-courage-to-be-a-fragment/.

Jones, S. M., R. Bailey, S. P. Barnes, and A. Partee. "Executive Function Mapping Project Untangling the Terms and Skills Related to Executive Function and Self-Regulation in Early Childhood." OPRE Report #2016-88, Washington, DC: Office of Planning, Research and Evaluation, Administration for Children and Families, U.S. Department of Health and Human Services, 2016.

Levine, Peter. *Waking the Tiger: Healing Trauma*. With Ann Frederick. Berkeley, CA: North Atlantic Books, 1997.

Palmer, Parker. *A Hidden Wholeness: The Journey Toward an Undivided Life*. San Francisco: Jossey-Bass, 2008.

Porges, Stephen. "The Polyvagal Theory: New Insights into Adaptive Reactions of the Autonomic Nervous System." *Cleveland Clinic Journal of Medicine* 76, suppl. 4 (June 2011): S86–S90. https://doi.org/10.3949/ccjm.76.s2.17.

Rosanbalm, K. D., and D. W Murray. "Co-Regulation from Birth through Young Adulthood: A Practice Brief" (OPRE Brief #2017-80). Washington, DC: Office of Planning, Research and Evaluation, Administration for Children and Families, U.S. Department of Health and Human Services, 2020 (2018).

Shore, Bradd. *The Hidden Powers of Ritual: The Journey of a Lifetime*. Cambridge, MA: MIT Press, 2023.

Steindl-Rast, David Brother. *The Way of Silence: Engaging the Sacred in Daily Life.* Cincinatti, OH: Franciscan Media, 2016.

Thurman, Howard. *Meditations of the Heart.* Boston: Beacon Press, 1999 (1953).

ENDNOTES

1. Common Worlds Research Collective, "Learning to Become *with* the World: Education for Future Survival," UNESCO (November 2020), https://unesdoc.unesco.org/ark:/48223/pf0000374923.
2. Stephen Porges, "The Polyvagal Theory"; Deb Dana, *Anchored*; Peter Levine, *Waking the Tiger*.
3. Linda Groves Gillespie, "Rocking and Rolling—It Takes Two."
4. Michaela Glöckler and Claudia Grah-Wittich, *The Dignity of the Young Child*, 73.
5. Haim G. Ginott, *Teacher and Child: A Book for Parents and Teachers* (New York: Macmillan, 1972), 13.
6. Margaret Atwood, "All Bread."
7. Josep Maria Esquirol, *The Intimate Resistance*.
8. I. and R. Heine, "Caring Is Education—Education Is Caring," in Glöckler and Grah-Wittich, 135–148.
9. Glöckler and Grah-Wittich, *Dignity of the Young Child*, 27.
10. Glöckler and Grah-Wittich.
11. See, e.g., Parker Palmer, *A Hidden Wholeness*.
12. "Open Invitations" in ibid., 78–80.

BECOMING AND BELONGING

3:
Beholding the Child
Laurie Clark

A four-year-old little boy, who had overheard a conversation from his older brother, wanted to explain something to me. He said, "Did you know that you have a brain that is on both sides of your head?"

"Hmm, I said, "How do you know that?"

He replied without any hesitation, "Because my angel helped build me, that's how I knowed."

be- (prefix): on, around, over; we might say, "on all sides, all around."

hold (verb): to grasp; we often use *hold* connoting to foster, to cherish, or to keep watch over.

behold (verb): while this literally means "to perceive in sight or apprehension," we also use it in the imperative, especially to call attention.

We derive a similar connotation from the Greek *eido* as it is used in the Bible, translated to English as "behold." *Eido* literally translates as *be sure to see*; we could also understand it as *don't miss this!*

Behold. Allow the eyes of the heart to be focused and enlightened.

beholder (noun): one who sees

BECOMING AND BELONGING

We also understand that the beholder experiences an awakening, an awareness of what they are looking at. To be a beholder you must pay attention, become a knower with your heart.

What mood do we need so that the eyes of our heart can open to a deeper perception that will allow us to "behold" a child? When we behold or contemplate a child, there is a fragile balance between our immediate impressions and what lies below the surface as a mystery yet to be revealed. Our commitment to this mood, on behalf of the developing child, helps us develop our capacities as teachers. When we share this work with our colleagues in a Caring Circle, it also enhances our sense of community with one another.

Janusz Korczak, a physician, educator, writer, and universal humanist, gives us some good advice in his books on how to care for children. He confesses at the beginning of one of his books: "I don't know anything. Readers who expect answers, put this book away. Those who are looking for questions are who this book is written for."[1]

Dr. Korczak speaks about absorbing the quality of the wondrous, creative "I don't know." He goes on to say that we must learn to love and take to heart this "I don't know" as a creative activity. As the Sufi poet Rumi says, "Sell your cleverness, buy bewilderment."[2]

Here are some important questions to consider when doing a child contemplation with a Caring Circle of teachers.

- Can I live with questions?
- Can I bear these questions in my heart?
- Can I let these questions have an effect on me?
- Can I find the language that is concealed within the child and let it speak to me?

The child is a riddle, partly known and partly unknown. Considering these wide-open questions can open up a wellspring of fresh understanding. Growing our own potential to observe precisely in this way leaves the child free. We can cultivate a renewed approach by developing an "inner seeing" with which to genuinely perceive the child. Mixing a blend of patience and openness, along with accepting that we will not know all of the answers right away, frees us from making hasty conclusions about a child. We can hold hope for what we do not know yet, bearing the questions with enthusiastic endurance. The old saying, "All good things take time" is advice to keep close. This soul mood can develop into a transformative sense organ that supports the child in their becoming.

Approaching the Mystery

> *"If you want a friend, tame me!"*
>
> *"What must I do to tame you?" asked the little prince.*
>
> *"You must be very patient," replied the fox. "First, you will sit down in the grass a little distance from me. I shall look at you out of the corner of my eye, and you will say nothing. Words are the source of misunderstandings. But every day, you will be able to sit a little closer to me."*
>
> —ANTOINE DE SAINT-EXUPÉRY, *The Little Prince*

Many of the "little friends" coming to us now are struggling. Children may have obstacles in their life path. Anxiety and stress, along with the fast pace of our world, can compromise the child's everyday experiences. But we can take the fox's clear instructions to the little prince about patience and the time and understanding it takes to approach him to heart, gives and reach out to these children with an empathetic attitude.

Henning Köhler, in his book *Working with Anxious, Nervous and Depressed Children,* says, "We must stand at the child's side with a waiting attitude, simply be there, patient."[3] Köhler gives us the same advice that the fox gives the Little Prince. True interest and attention know how to wait.

There are an increasing number of children today who have difficulties feeling at home in their bodies. Often this presents itself as a disturbance in the child's foundational senses. Instability in the senses of touch, balance, and self-movement can shake a child's sense of well-being. Trauma can shake a child's confidence in existence so that the ways of the world simply do not make sense.

Other children seem to carry a kind of restless search for something they cannot quite grasp or take hold of. They seem dissatisfied and needy. They seem to suffer from some sort of lack—a coldness that needs warming, a trauma that needs healing, a trust that needs to be reestablished, or some other mystery yet to be discovered. These children can also exhibit an extraordinary strength of will. Yet, often, their will can be obscured by fear, defiance, and even a deep sorrow springing from their essential being. This veil of aberrant behavior often masks a noble destiny.

Every human being is on a pilgrimage, a wanderer who has come to the earth with purpose, resolve, and a mission to fulfill. We are walking on sacred ground here and must tread with a humble footing. With each encounter, we have the opportunity to take in the child's situation with an open heart and all the depth of our capacities.

Forming a Caring Circle

What does it mean to focus and give our deep interest to one young human being? Should we call this process a child study? "Study" means a devotion of time and attention to acquiring knowledge on an academic subject. If we carefully consider our words in describing the practice of giving dedicated time and conscious effort to understanding a child, a more accurate term would be the word "contemplation."

> contemplation (noun): an act of considering with attention; the act of regarding steadily

Perhaps the "contemplation" describes our intentions more accurately than "study" in trying to form a supportive companionship with the child.

Chapter 3: Beholding the Child

When the decision is made to contemplate and hold a child in community, a compassionate circle of teachers comes together who want to behold, guide, and become active on the child's behalf. If we work together out of generosity and love for a child, we model the realm of the angels. In a way, we are emulating what the angels do in utmost selflessness for us. But this kind of process can only be accomplished through intensive commitment among those teachers who are 'beholding' the child. The ultimate question may be, what does it feel like to be this child? A raw openness is needed as the community of teachers holds an inner mirror that reflects back to them the child's situation.

When we strive to contemplate the child, we must become radically honest with ourselves as educators and ask what it is we might need to overcome in ourselves. Is there something holding us back from finding our way to the child? Do we have a complete and utter "yes-ness," an unconditional acceptance of the child? Do we have the kind of "yes-ness" that starts where the child is and not where we wish them to be?

Can we take into consideration the intentions that the child so earnestly brings? Original intentions have to do with the essence of the will in each individual human being and the resolve to incarnate and integrate the heavenly into the earthly with the help of higher powers. The original intentions we all carry shine above us as a star that guides us on our way. The Three Kings followed the most radiant star to find the Christmas child and bring their sacramental offerings. Rudolf Steiner stated in a lecture on the three Magi, "To be led by a star means nothing else than to see the soul itself as a star."[4] How can we find the sacramental mirror in ourselves that will lead us to recognize the child's star? What gifts will we have to offer? What gifts is the child bringing?

This verse by Herbert Hahn, a teacher in the first Waldorf School, might be helpful to prepare the contemplative mood in a Caring Circle:

> It will indeed come to be for us a necessity
> That we observe the children day by day
> And also exercise in ourselves day by day
> Control of our own thoughts and feelings.
> Every child has a subtle perception
> Of whether the person looking after him [her]
> Or teaching him (her) is inwardly equipped in their soul
> The child's well-being depends to a great extent
> On what is growing and developing in the inner soul
> Of the person in charge.
> Develop your keenness of observation;
> Nurture the powers of your inner Being;
> Develop vitality of thinking;
> Depth of feeling, strength of willing.

This verse is an amazing one to contemplate when beginning to look into the world of the child. It is so very interesting that Herbert Hahn would emphasize that the child's well-being depends upon the inner striving of the teacher. It is true that when we try to understand and contemplate the child, we are immediately faced with the question of whether genuine perceptions can be born in us that will give us the possibility of accompanying the child on their journey, or as Henning Köhler so eloquently states when talking about the child, as "the guest looking for the way."[5]

Nonjudgmental objectivity needs to be paired with reverential attention. All naming and psychologizing of symptoms and behaviors must be laid aside in the minds of the teachers so that the inspiration waiting to be heard behind these symptoms and behaviors can be recognized. This kind of hearing is planted like a seed in the hearts of educators. It is as if one were trying to listen to what the child's angel is revealing to us.

After this initial gesture of listening has taken place, a living imagination of the child's situation may arise. Through the Child Contemplation

Chapter 3: Beholding the Child

Process, colleagues who are part of the Caring Circle share their observations and images, and together, the group can begin to create a healing picture. Often the children who come to us have obstacles on their life path and are calling for our unreserved help.

At every step on this journey, we need to ask ourselves: Is the process becoming frozen with too many set concepts? Is the process becoming too rigid and formulaic or too loose with no form at all? When holding a human being in the warm embrace of a group of teachers, it is essential to make sure the process remains active and alive.

Unfolding the Contemplation—Some Aspects to Consider

The *Calendar of the Soul* by Rudolf Steiner is a helpful place to begin. There is a verse for every week of the year, which can be matched to the child's birth week. This suggests a kind of spiritual geography, the essence of the time the child chose to be born.[6]

The etymology of "observe" is interesting. The original Latin is *observare*, which literally means "to watch over." True observation means to keep safe and protect the child before us. Enkindling deep observation cultivates interest in the child; everything about the child asks for our attention. The way the child moves, the way the child doesn't move, the sound of their voice, their gestures, everything! Each day we can notice something our senses did not show us the day before. Look at the child. What stands out for you? Notice everything about the child; nothing is unimportant.

Rudolf Steiner indicates that through the intensive study of the physical configuration of the body, characteristics of the soul are revealed. To take a deep interest in the physical description of the child with an absolute "devotion to little things" is enthusiastically emphasized by Steiner. He says, "We must not omit to cultivate this interest in very little things. The tip of the ear, the paring of a fingernail, a single human hair—should be every bit as interesting to us as Saturn, Sun and Moon."[7]

BECOMING AND BELONGING

Can we observe in such a way that after we watch the child move, we can imitate the movement, feel it in our own body, and begin to sense and experience what it feels like to be that child? Looking from the outside and observing the child and then bringing what is seen into one's own experience may guide us to an insightful understanding. Can we walk just like the child does, imitate their facial expressions to see what that feels like? Here we are doing what the child does for us; they imitate us unconsciously. We imitate the child's movements consciously to see what it feels like to be them. Bringing into our own body what the child does will speak to us and give us impressions of their true self.

Behaviors give an interesting perspective. Every behavior is a communication to the teacher; through their behavior, the children are often trying to tell us something. Tantrums can express feeling totally overwhelmed, refusal could possibly be triggered by a fear of doing what is being asked or extreme anxiety. Every behavior speaks to us. We can ask, "What is the child trying to tell us beneath the behavior they are exhibiting?"

Paying special attention to when the behaviors occur can also be revealing. Are they falling apart before snack because their blood sugar has dropped? Or is a child refusing to do what is asked at transitions because of high anxiety? Every behavior that the child exhibits is valuable in gaining a deeper perception.

With children seven years old and younger, considering how the four foundational senses of touch, self-movement, balance, and well-being live in the child can give us much-needed information (see chapter 4 for a fuller treatment of the foundational senses.)

Observing how the child plays gives us a deeper sense of their inner life. What do they like to play? Do they prefer to play alone or does the child invite others to participate in their play? Do they prefer, during creative playtime, to talking to adults?

Listen to the child's voice. Does it seem too loud or too soft? Harmonious? How is their articulation, the flow of breath? Does the voice have a high or low pitch? Do they gasp for air as they speak? Stutter? Elongate words? Rudolf Steiner is quoted, in *The Therapeutic Eye* by Peter Selg, as telling us how beneficial it is for the teacher to train their own hearing as they listen to the voice of the child. He goes on to say that we can spiritually train our hearing so that when we listen to the child speak, we can begin to grasp insight into the essential nature of the child.[8]

If the teacher can have a conversation with the parents, then that information can add a more comprehensive view of the child. It is always interesting to know as much as possible about the sleeping and waking life of the child. These two thresholds, between sleep and waking, hold many mysteries and give hints about the constitution of the child. Is the child a restless or a light sleeper, or does she sleep so soundly that she is hard to wake? Does she chirp like a little bird, happy in the morning and ready for breakfast upon waking, or is she edgy, nervous, and unable to eat until later? The kind of sleep a child has or does not have deeply affects how their day is lived out. Nutrition is also a key factor in the behavior and energy of the child and can be quite significant.

Another thing to consider—Is there a fairy tale that describes the child's life situation? When we picture where the child is and bring our imagination to that picture, we may find a fairytale that connects with the child's soul. It can give an image of where the child is, symbolically, on their journey. Is the child in a hollow tree? Is the child hiding in the clock case? Did their golden ball just fall into the well? (See the section on fairy tales in chapter 12.) Another way to work symbolically, for example, would be to see the child as an image from nature.

The first part of the contemplation occurs at the first meeting of the Caring Circle. It is advisable to continue with a second session within a few days or a week. Taking this pause allows all of these impressions to be taken into our sleep. All of the necessary ingredients—the observations, the listening, and the empathetic engagement in the process—are brought together.

BECOMING AND BELONGING

We can ask for assistance from our spiritual helpers so that what we have gathered may be transformed into a deeper understanding. "Sleep is the little brother of death," it is said, and if we can bring our thoughts of the child into sleep with us, we open ourselves to the possibility of inspiration. This activity can create a hallowed space in our souls, a kind of safe, inner manger where the child's being can find the way to us.

The second session can begin with sharing the impressions of the child that came out of this work in sleep life. Then the biography and developmental milestones of the child can be shared. The reason the biographical information is not shared before this time is that it often tends to color the picture of the child so strongly that it may affect the open-mindedness needed during the descriptive contemplation and the sleep work. It may cause us to jump to conclusions too soon before receiving and penetrating our observations. Assessments or screenings that have been done can be presented along with the child's drawings. Then as many threads that have been gathered are woven together into a tapestry that offers the possibility of leading the teacher to what Henning Köhler calls true "inner accompaniment."

At this stage of the process, suggestions and ideas are discussed. It may be that no definite solutions are offered. But the teacher stands by the child with a revived and renewed effort. Even when there are no concrete ideas, we remember that solutions are not the primary goal of the contemplation. It is out of the inner effort of the teachers involved in the contemplation, and their striving to expand and stretch their own being to make room for the child, that new understanding can arise. It is as if the child's star begins to shine inside of us. It is through the grace of this activity that we can now gaze back at the child with a new perspective that allows the child a free space in which to move and grow.

The contemplation can close with the Calendar of the Soul or whatever verse the Caring Circle would like to bring. A few quiet moments after this are always welcome to digest this process and to send gratitude to the child and to all who participated.[9]

The verse by Herbert Hahn, in the section "Forming a Caring Circle," is well known in Waldorf circles, having been passed from teacher to teacher for years. Herbert Hahn taught at the first Waldorf School in Stuttgart, Germany (from Wikipedia, https://en.wikipedia.org/wiki/Herbert_Hahn).

ENDNOTES

1. Janutz Korczak, *How to Love a Child and Other Selected Works*, vol. 1. (Chicago: Vallentine Mitchell, 2018). Dr. Korczak was an educator and pediatrician who devoted his whole life to the care of children. He wrote children's books and books for adults that had to do with the care of children. He established an orphanage for Jewish children in Warsaw, Poland. During the years of the Nazi's rise to power, Korczak bravely sheltered his two hundred children from the brutality of the Warsaw Ghetto until the Nazis forced him to lead the orphans to the Treblinka death camp. When a Nazi soldier at Treblinka offered to spare Korczak from extermination, he refused and remained with his children until the end; see Betty Jean Lifton, *The King of Children: The Life and Death of Janusz Korczak* (Elk Grove Village, IL: American Academy of Pediatrics, 2005).

2. Jalāl al-Dīn Rūmī, *The Essential Rumi*, translated by Coleman Banks (Edison, NJ: Castle Books, 1997).

3. Henning Köhler, *Working with Anxious, Nervous and Depressed Children: A Spiritual Perspective to Guide Parents* (Fair Oaks, CA: Association of Waldorf Schools of North America, 2000), 128.

4. Rudolf Steiner, *The Three Wise Men: And the Birth of Jesus* (Forest Row, England: Rudolf Steiner Press, 2017), 90.

5. Henning Köhler, *Difficult Children—There Is No Such Thing: An Appeal for the Transformation of Educational Thinking* (Fair Oaks, CA: Association of Waldorf Schools of North America, 2003), 121.

6. Rudolf Steiner, *The Calendar of the Soul* (Hudson, NY: SteinerBooks, 2023).

7. Rudolf Steiner, *Education for Special Needs: The Curative Education Course* (Forest Row, UK: Rudolf Steiner Press, 2014), 124.

8. Peter Selg, *The Therapeutic Eye: How Rudolf Steiner Observed Children* (Hudson, NY: SteinerBooks, 2008), 46.

9. Please see appendices II and III in this volume, "A Potent Tool for Waldorf Schools in Challenging Times" and "Sevenfold Path: An Outline for Child Contemplation."

BECOMING AND BELONGING

4:
Sensory Development as the Foundation for a Healthy Social-Emotional Life

Nancy Blanning

The children spotted some sturdy cardboard packing boxes in the school common room with a nice slick floor. Instantly a child climbed into each box, just the right size to be an individual boat, train, or race car. Other children instinctively got behind each box and pushed with all their might. The now repurposed "vehicles" careened across the floor with squeals of delight and laughter. The passengers were jiggled and joggled as the boxes swerved across the floor and the wagon bumped along the ground. A good time was had by all. A natural body wisdom guided the children. To push and pull, to feel pressure in the limbs, to feel the supportive resistance of the earth reassures and strengthens the experience of "I am!"

When casual observers look into a Waldorf early childhood classroom, they encounter an environment with beautiful aesthetics formed by soft, inviting colors and natural materials. If children are in the room, they are playing if not otherwise engaged by circle-time movement and imagination, story-telling, and different sorts of practical and artistic activities. It appears sweet and nurturing—which it is. These activities are not an end in themselves, however. Each is a stepping stone to support human development toward building strong, healthy social and emotional lives for each individual student and the class as a whole. This commitment is one of the profound intentions that undergirds Waldorf education throughout the entire curriculum. In subtle and obvious ways, the curriculum focuses on building relationships in multiple dimensions—relationship of oneself to the physical body, relationship to the natural world, and relationship to other human beings.

The beginning of Waldorf education was planted in a moment of strife, when much of political, economic, moral, and social life was in shambles, in the aftermath of World War I. Emil Molt, a student of Rudolf Steiner familiar with the ideas of the Three-fold Social Order, asked the long-awaited question. Did Steiner have ideas of an education that would encourage humanity toward a healing, healthy social life with more respectful and caring, tolerant, empathetic, and justice-filled creative thinking to guide how we live with one another? Waldorf education is the answer to that question.

Educational circles are currently buzzing with conversation about social and emotional education. One sees curricula for purchase that offer early childhood educators discrete lessons for teaching social-emotional skills. Waldorf early education from its inception has intrinsically offered opportunities to grow social-emotional capacities through each day's experiences.

Steiner perceived that children come to earthly life with anticipation of being recognized as beings of body, soul, and spirit. Understanding this was one of the first principles that Rudolf Steiner articulated in the 1919 pedagogical lectures given to the soon-to-be teachers of the first Waldorf School.[1] He emphasized that the developing human being is an entity with this threefold nature. Anatomy and physiology describe and "explain" the body. Psychology explores emotional life—a step toward acknowledgement of soul—but too often from a cold, clinical perspective. Steiner's understanding of the human being opens a wider picture. Steiner spoke to teachers as follows:

> When we perceive the children with our physical eyes once they are born, we need to remember that their earthly life, too, is a continuation ... our physical earthly existence is the continuation of a former spiritual life; and that as educators we continue the work higher beings previously did without our help. Our teaching will be imbued with the right mood if we bear this in mind: in working with [these children] I am continuing the work done by higher beings before [the children were] born.[2]

> If ... we realize that our tasks as teachers are connected to a human soul that steps into earthly existence and, from hour-to-hour and week-to-week, increasingly develops its inner capacities, *and if we stand before a growing human being as before a sacred riddle to be solved, a being who has come to us from the endless distances of the cosmos so that we can give that being the possibility to unfold and develop, then many new tasks, outlooks, and possibilities will arise for all of human life.*[3]

The individuality newly born into physical life comes with a biography carried along from the spiritual world. There, previous experiences have been reviewed, sorted, pondered upon, digested, and then carried with insight into an incarnation with a new life plan. It is said that each human being comes into earthly life with intentions and resolves that can only be fulfilled in this time, place, physical body, culture, and social circumstances. There are people to meet and things to do. Individuals return in a new incarnation to fulfill a new life plan in interactions with other human beings, to enter into human social encounter. Fostering healthy social life is one of Waldorf education's intentions. The social encounter with the teacher can be positive and encouraging when the teacher appreciates that these children come with a long story behind them. The child is, indeed, a "sacred riddle" to be accepted and respected.

BECOMING AND BELONGING

The child takes on a physical body with inherited aspects and physical inclinations. We are all familiar with this inherited part. There are also aspects brought from the spiritual world, carried by the unseen spirit-soul body, that need to join harmoniously with the physical-life body we can see.

However, these two parts do not automatically or easily integrate with each other.

An unbiased observer will notice, as the children grow into the world, that their spirit-soul is not yet fully connected with the bodily organism. Spiritually speaking, it is the task of education to bring the two together into a harmonious whole, because, when the child is first born into the physical body, the two are to some extent not yet attuned to one another. As teachers we have to facilitate this process.[4]

This union has never been easy, but in our current times it is becoming harder and harder for the soul-spirit to come into harmonious, cooperative relationship with the physical life-body. The phenomena of restless, fidgety nervousness, and anxiety displayed in children by disharmonious movement and dysregulated behavior has been growing and growing. The pandemic years intensified the challenges children display in finding comfort in their bodies and peacefulness in mind and heart. More than ever, the child is a "sacred riddle" or mystery standing before us. Where do we begin to carry on the work that higher beings guided before the children were born? When and how do we escort them into social life?

The Role of Sensory Development

This is where the role of the senses steps into the forefront of our attention and appreciation. It is through the senses, primarily the foundational four senses of touch, well-being, self-movement, and balance, that the soul-spirit and the life-bodily contributions are integrated.

Chapter 4: Sensory Development as the Foundation for Healthy Social-Emotional Life

The spiritual world has sent to us the blessing of these children. And, fortunately, it has also sent each human being with twelve senses as gifts carried by the physical body. These senses are gateways to finding one's way into earthly life. When these senses work together in reliable, mutually supportive ways, they tell us about our own bodies; about the external, created world; and about other people.

Understanding these twelve senses allows us as educators to better behold the child. When we learn to appreciate the importance of each sense and observe how each sense serves the child, we have twelve new windows allowing us to look into the child's personal experience of the world and sense of comfort and security in living in the physical body. It is well known that feeling secure, comfortable, competent, and confident in the physical body is a prerequisite for a healthy social and emotional life. The strength of the four foundational senses are the cornerstones for this secure, happily inhabited physical body.

A general description from an anthroposophical perspective of the influence and experience each sense provides is helpful here. Steiner had pondered the physical, social, and spiritual importance of each sense over decades and arrived at this listing of the twelve, starting with *touch, life* or *well-being, self-movement, balance, smell, taste, sight, warmth,* and *hearing*. These first nine are more or less familiar to us. But the sensory list goes further to include three more. There is also a sense through which we recognize and understand language, named the sense of *word* or *speech*. Another sense enables us to grasp the *thoughts* and *concepts* of the other person. And the crowning sense is one by which we can recognize and acknowledge the *"I"-being* of another person. The list below shows how Steiner presented the senses to the first teachers according to an order in which recognizing the "I"-being of the other is at the top as the highest spiritual sense, while the sense of touch, at the bottom of the list, appears as the first foundational sense.

Highest/Social/Spiritual Senses

- "I"-being—sensing the humanity and individuality of another; sensing the "I"-being of another person.

- Thought—recognizing that words expressed by other people are sequenced to convey thoughts and concepts; perceiving the thoughts of other people.

- Word/Language/Speech—sensing that sounds, hand movement, or gestures in particular sequences convey meaning. Sense of word takes sound (or hand gesture, i.e., sign language) and gives it meaning.

- Hearing—experiencing sound through the mechanism of the ear. Attentively focused hearing is listening.

Middle/Feeling Senses

- Warmth—sensing temperature as warmer or cooler in comparison to our own body temperature.

- Sight—taking in visual impressions through the eyes, connected to light.

- Taste—experiencing sweet, bitter, salty, and sour by taking in substances through the mouth with help of the watery element (saliva).

- Smell—experiencing the outer world through the airy element in smells, aromas.

FOUNDATIONAL/WILL SENSES

- Balance/Equilibrium—sensing uprightness and body position in relation to the earth and gravity.

- Self-movement/Proprioception—sensing the cooperative movement of one's limbs and coordination, learning body geography.

- Life or Well-Being—sensing the health and balance of inner organic life.
- Touch—experiencing the boundary between self and world.

Through the first foundational senses of touch, life or well-being, self-movement, and balance, we experience overall well-being and stability, reliability of posture, and coordination of our own physical bodies as we relate to the earth's gravity.

The middle or feeling senses—smell, taste, sight, and warmth—give us information about the nature and qualities of things external to ourselves in the world. Experiences through these senses often result in feelings of sympathy or antipathy toward what we encounter—do I like it or not?

The third group of senses, called the social, highest, and even spiritual senses, stands as new identifications of subtle sensing capacities inherent within each human being. Through these, we can recognize and come into relationship with other human beings. These senses are the familiar sense of hearing and newly described senses of recognizing meaning through word and gesture, recognizing meaning and concept in the thought of another, and sensing the "I"-being of other human beings.

Young children, from birth to the change of teeth, are working to form, grow, and strengthen their physical bodies. Waldorf education sees this as the fundamental task of the first seven years as children strive to claim ownership of and find comfort in their bodies through posture, movement, coordination, and speech, for example. During these years, children also make the first steps into social life, using their senses to encounter others who are also on their own sensing journeys to find their place and purposefulness in the world.

Supporting Healthy Sensory Development Is an Essential Educational Responsibility

Supporting healthy development of the foundational senses is a primary educational responsibility for Waldorf early childhood teachers. These senses are engaged through movement. Current neurological research now confirms that physical gross and fine motor movement and building of neurological pathways are related. What is accomplished in neurological development through movement (especially well-ordered, purposeful, rhythmically repeated movement) and opportunity to explore the environment in the first seven years prepares the foundation for future cognitive, emotional, and social life.

The importance of these senses cannot be overemphasized. As we understand and appreciate how vital these are to the child's immediate and long-term development, observing each sensory domain opens up a new window through which we can behold and appreciate the child.

~

Touch, or the tactile sense, is the first to be awakened. In the birth process, strong uterine contractions massage the baby and awaken and tune up the sense of touch. When touch is under-stimulated, sometimes through a C-section delivery, or from lying naked in an incubator as a "preemie," the child may be touch sensitive. What is a normal touch experience for most of us can feel like an assault to this child. The child will avoid typical exploration of the world through touch, and is often fussy and finicky about clothes, textures, and temperature.

On the other extreme, if the tactile sense has been overtaxed by overstimulation at a critical developmental moment, the child's touch sense may shut down in a gesture of self-protection. Such a child may be unaware that he has touched another child, that his hands are crusted with sand and mud, or that his shoes are on the wrong feet. One often hears complaints from other children, such as, "She is holding my hand too tight," while the child who is doing this is not aware of her friend's experience. Steiner explains that touch gives us our experience of boundary, telling us where we stop and where the rest of the world begins. A healthy sense of touch lays the foundation for a sense of social boundaries as well.

We support and educate the sense of touch in the early childhood classroom through kneading bread dough, washing dishes and cloths, digging in the sand box, touching different textures and natural materials, and so on. In circle work we also strengthen the sense of touch, encouraging more touch tolerance for the too-sensitive extreme and more touch awareness at the opposite, under-responsive pole. Holding hands with other children, crawling on the floor with an open palm, feeling the length of the body when rolling or tummy crawling on the floor, and walking in soft soles over uneven river stones are all strengthening and integrating to the sense of touch.

~

Through the *sense of life* we experience our organic well-being. We become aware of this general sense when the body is disturbed by feeling unwell or out of sorts. Our awareness of this sense is usually asleep when all is calm and tranquil. Disturbances in the life sense demonstrate themselves in the child's rhythmic life of waking and sleeping, eating and elimination. In the classroom we encounter difficulties here with food allergies and narrow, restricted dietary choices. Children with a diminished or disturbed life sense may lack vitality and cannot participate with true enthusiasm in many of life's activities. The strong rhythms we maintain in the kindergarten through each day and week are essential in supporting the life sense.

The life sense is supported in movement work as well. Improved sense of balance helps to heighten a sense of well-being. Some children with hypersensitive balance may actually feel vaguely motion-sick all the time. Since it is how they always feel, however, they do not know that this is unusual. Strengthening balance gives the child an experience of standing on the earth more securely and confidently. When balance works harmoniously with the other senses, an improved sense of well-being results. Feeling more secure in this realm, the child develops better tolerance for other things in life. This may include becoming more venturesome in trying new foods and expanding one's diet. Supported by improved nutrition, the life sense is further fostered.

~

The *sense of self-movement*, or proprioceptive sense, gives us awareness of our own body position. It informs where our body parts are in relation to one another. It also gives us the framework for developing body geography. Information about the body's position is provided by the contracting, stretching, and compression of muscles and tendons in the joints. Without a healthy sense of proprioception, the child may truly be unaware of where their limbs are in space, sincerely incredulous that an arm has just "struck" another child or knocked down a classmate's house. Healthy proprioception provides the ability to begin and arrest movement with control. Holding appropriate muscle tension in a task, such as lifting up a glass of water with the right force, comes from this sense. Sustaining upright posture is also a function of proprioception. With difficulty here, often a child would collapse onto the floor at circle time, as standing upright is such a chore. Children who often bump into objects and other people, who seem a little clumsy, or who slump or collapse may have difficulty with self-movement/proprioception.

Children find support for this sense whenever they experience tension or pressure in the joints and limbs. Carrying a heavy stump, pulling a wagon loaded with classmates, hanging from a bar, swinging on a trapeze, pushing or pulling something heavy, jumping, hopping, and being on the bottom of a pile of other children all stimulate and satisfy the need for proprioceptive input. The child whose sense is weak will crave these kinds of activities. In movement work, starting and stopping with control ("galloping horses" then " whoa!"), kicking up their heels like a donkey, walking on hands as a "wheelbarrow," holding up the feet and legs of another child to wheel him as a "wheelbarrow," jumping, hopping, jumping off a table or tree stump, or touching and naming body parts in an imagination (to strengthen an experience of body geography) all strengthen the sense of self-movement.

~

Balance, or the vestibular sense, gives the experience of stability and security in relation to gravity. Working along with proprioception, the vestibular sense tells where the body is in space. The vestibular sensory organs, the semicircular canals, lie within the complex of the inner ear. Chronic ear infections place auditory and vestibular health under attack. This may be one reason why we see many children with vestibular insecurity in our classes. Children are also commonly deprived of chances to move freely so they can experience their bodies in space, or to take chances because of adults' fearfulness about injury.

Children with vestibular weakness can be of two extremes. They can be very movement sensitive, avoiding spinning, swinging, inverting the head, all of which stimulate the vestibular system. They avoid movement. On the other extreme are children who crave movement at all times. They spin on the tire swing and never get dizzy. They fidget and rock in their chairs. They may be daredevils who lack an appropriate sense of caution. The vestibular sense of these children is under-responsive, requiring a constant stream of stimulus to keep them informed of where the body's center of balance lies. The importance of this sense cannot be over emphasized. A. Jean Ayres, in *Sensory Integration and the Child*, states that the vestibular is the unifying system that provides a framework for other aspects of our experience. It seems to "prime" the entire nervous system to function effectively.

A kindergarten equipped with swings, a tire swing, landscaping timbers or logs to walk along and balance on, rocks and stumps of uneven heights to climb over, trees or play structures to climb, hills for sledding or rolling, and slides to whiz down offers healthy possibilities for vestibular stimulation. In general, balance is stimulated whenever anyone swings, spins, slides quickly down an incline, lowers or inverts the head, or goes around and around in a circle. Walking on a beam, whether leveled on the floor or inclined, challenges the balance, as does walking on uneven river stones. Circling in a ring, spinning by oneself or with a partner, turning, and twisting also provide the right kind of stimulation. You will all see all of these used extensively in the movement experiences designed to emphasize strengthening of the foundational senses.[5]

Healthy sensory development has been increasingly challenged in recent decades, particularly by the prevalence of screens and other distractions that keep children from knowing the world through movement and free, child-directed exploration. These restrictions deprive children of the opportunity to develop themselves. When we now see children's restlessness, agitation, and anxiety, a study of the senses opens our eyes to a more compassionate understanding of what children are dealing with. Observing the health or distress of sensory systems gives clues to what children need in order to feel secure and confident in their bodies, a basic requirement for social-emotional health.

Transformation—From Foundational Senses to Metamorphosed Social-Emotional Capacities

Regarding social-emotional development, the anthroposophical view of the Foundational Senses reaches even deeper and more profoundly into aspects beyond physical life. In his study and spiritual research into human "twelveness," Rudolf Steiner also recognized that there are direct connections between pairs of senses. Specifically, he noted that the four basic senses of touch, life, self-movement, and balance have individual relationships to the four highest senses of ego, thought, speech/word, and hearing (these upper four are deliberately reversed in this listing, as will be explained.) The four basic senses establish the foundation for the all of human development. Through these basic four, we are able to come to uprightness, speech, and thinking.[6] These accomplishments are essential for being able to enter into social life as well. Through movement, listening, speaking, and acknowledging the being of the other person, we become social beings. The first four senses provide the foundation upon which not only physical but social life is formed. Each of the highest senses is a transformation and nonphysical metamorphosis of a foundational sense. The pairs are:

Sensing the "I"-being of another is a metamorphosis of touch

Sensing the thought of another is a metamorphosis of the sense of life/well-being

Sensing the word of another is a metamorphosis of self-movement

Directed hearing expands itself to become listening as a metamorphosis of balance

The important implication here is that the health and strength of each of these highest senses depends directly upon how fully and reliably its partner foundational sense has developed.[7] Strongly developed foundational senses are a prerequisite for the possibility of healthy, sensitive, adept social senses. Deliberate, intentional, aware attention to the foundational senses in the child's first seven years becomes even more crucial as a pedagogical priority when we appreciate this long-term view.

One More Big Step Toward Social-Emotional Growth

These alone are big guidelines to consider. Yet there is one more step we can suggest to support this human structure of body, soul, and spirit. We sometimes experience how our response to sensory stimuli affects our emotional and psychological state. If our body systems are working in balanced ways, we tend to feel optimistic and tolerant. If we don't feel well, we may withdraw and feel "touchy," sensitive, irritable. If we feel overwhelmed by too much noise, crowding, demands for our attention and energies, we may find ourselves feeling self-defensive, intolerant of daily ups and downs, and lacking an attitude of generosity and gratitude to life and to other people. Rudolf Steiner and other researchers after him, particularly Henning Köhler, have looked deeply into the correlation between sensory health and states of soul—our feelings and states of mind.

Henning Köhler, in his book *Working with Anxious, Nervous, and Depressed Children*, describes the virtues and positive outlook that accompany each healthy foundational sense. He also observed accompanying states of distress when the basic sense has not unfolded in a healthy, reliable way that serves the child. Köhler develops a full picture of these relationships in his study. Below is a summary of these correlations. The positive virtues of a healthily developed sense are a joy to see. And the counterpole of emotional distress is commonly seen in our times. Köhler sees the senses of self-movement and balance as so intimately connected that he treats them as an indivisible pair when considering the virtues. While noting the particular virtues of self-movement and balance, he sees that the child with a "brooding" disposition will benefit from receiving attention to both senses at the same time.

Henning Köhler—Working with Anxious, Nervous, and Depressed Children

Sensory Domain	Virtue If Well Developed	Emotional Distress If Underdeveloped
BALANCE	EQUANIMITY JUSTICE	BROODING, DEPRESSION
SELF-MOVEMENT	COMPASSION TACTFULNESS	
LIFE/WELL-BEING	TOLERANCE PATIENCE REVERENCE	NERVOUSNESS
TOUCH	TRUST SELFLESSNESS TRUE CARING FOR OTHERS	ANXIETY

Presented by Nancy Blanning at "Movement Toward Tolerance," a workshop hosted by the Waldorf Early Childhood Association of North America in February 2022. Note that Köhler observes the influential link between self-movement and balance, which reveals itself in similar expressions of distress.

Henning Köhler was an advocate for children:

> [A] compassionate approach should be the prevailing one all through children's schooling! It too often happens that an awkward, timid, or confused child is taken to task, in a moralizing tone, for being lazy or for being deliberately obstructive or ill-behaved.
>
> There is no such thing as a deliberately mean, lazy, or rebellious child! Every one of them longs from the bottom of their heart to do well

and to be praised for it. It is we who turn them into lazybones and rebels by reproaching them in their need.[8]

He observed that difficult, perplexing behaviors often arise out of stalled, "stuck," or insufficient sensory development. Children look to their caregivers to offer a pathway toward health because their current environments are not providing what they need.

If we picture that healthy foundational senses metamorphose into healthy social senses, we can picture how the positive virtues associated with each sense accompany the actual sensory capacities. Trust, tolerance, compassion, and a sense for justice and equanimity become available as social virtues with the healthy development of these senses. Working with children in through movement, as discussed above, is working foundationally and subtly to develop trust, tolerance, compassion, and a sense for justice and equanimity in social encounters.

Yet Köhler also observes that, to the contrary, when the senses are insufficiently developed, negative qualities of anxiousness and timidity, nervousness, broodiness, depression, disappointment, and cynicism arise. These antisocial expressions of suspicion, distrust, fearfulness, defensiveness, restlessness, and intolerance are a worldwide phenomenon of our time. In considering these associations, we can open a door to a healthy social life through focused work with the senses.

Waldorf education is based upon this unique picture of child development. Experience comes first through the physical body. When the physical body is sufficiently mature, the human being ventures out into the world and begins developing a conscious feeling life. And finally, trust and security in the world achieved through the body senses become social and emotional virtues and capacities in wider human encounters. Rudolf Steiner has often been credited with the aphorism that we cannot understand anything conceptually that we have not experienced through the bodily and feeling senses first. Children sense their way into uprightness through touch, self-movement, and balance. The life sense experiences ease and comfort in regular body rhythms and these other three senses give the child feelings of security in the physical body.

We can also understand that the first three great accomplishments—standing, speaking, and thinking—are socially dependent. These can only be achieved when there is a human imitative model. These first achievements are literally the first steps toward social life. A healthy social life is the ultimate destination for the human community. We want to make each step strong. What comes first physically prepares the way for the subtle and superior goals of social life, as this unique understanding shared by Steiner reveals. Physical security, emotional stability, and social harmony begin with the young child's movement. Healthy development of the foundational senses lays the groundwork for what is possible in emotional inner stability, equanimity, and social tolerance for the child's whole of life. We are working to support humanity's social future every time we hop, skip, dance, spin, sing, and jump for joy.

REFERENCES

Aeppli, Willi. *The Care and Development of the Human Senses.* Translated by Valerie Freilich. Edinburgh: Floris Books, 1996.

Ayres, A. Jean. *Sensory Integration and the Child: Understanding Hidden Sensory Challenges.* Los Angeles: Western Psychological Services, 1995.

Blanning, Nancy and Laurie Clark. *Movement Journeys and Circle Adventures.* Volume 1. Published by the authors, 2006.

———. *Movement Journeys and Circle Adventures.* Volume 2. Published by the authors, 2016.

Köhler, Henning. *Working with Anxious, Nervous, and Depressed Children: A Spiritual Perspective to Guide Parents.* Fair Oaks, CA: Association of Waldorf Schools of North America, 2000.

Steiner, Rudolf. *The Child's Changing Consciousness.* Hudson, NY: Anthroposophic Press, 1996.

Steiner, Rudolf. *The First Teachers' Course.* Translated by Margot Saar. Edited by Neil Boland and Jon McAlice. Bangkok, Thailand: Ratayakom, 2019.

Steiner, Rudolf. "Predisposition, Talent and Education of the Human Being." Lecture given in Berlin, Germany, January 12, 1911, GA 60. Published at the Rudolf Steiner Archive. https://rsarchive.org/Lectures/GA060/English/eLib2015/19110112p01.html.

ENDNOTES

1. Rudolf Steiner, *The First Teachers' Course*, 21–22.
2. Ibid.
3. Rudolf Steiner, "Predisposition, Talent and Education of the Human Being," 12; emphasis added.
4. Steiner, *First Teachers' Course*, 23.
5. Nancy Blanning and Laurie Clark, *Movement Journeys and Circle Adventures*, vol. 2, 8–10.
6. Rudolf Steiner, *The Child's Changing Consciousness*, lectures 1–4.
7. This is described in many of Rudolf Steiner's lectures and by other authors as well, notably Willi Aeppli, in *The Care and Development of the Human Senses*.
8. Henning Köhler, *Working with Anxious, Nervous, and Depressed Children*, 122.

5:
Re-Membering Play
Stephanie Hoelscher

Let all things be where thou art, childlike ever.
—GOETHE, "TRILOGY OF PASSION"

Once upon a time, a teacher remembers, two little boys, long-time competitors, both wanted to be king of the castle. They stood on a table where each declared himself king. The teacher, Joan Almon, walked past quietly muttering to herself, "There was once a country that had two kings." The play at once opened up to new possibilities.

The literature on play is vast and deep. Play, recognized as a hallmark of life, brings together psychologists, scientists, animal biologists, educators, mystics, urban planners, and poets. This vast web of interconnecting thought also comes together when we see that play provides the work and will for the future. Linger on that for a moment.

Pretend that you, as teacher, are holding the space for a parent gathering. You bring a warming, imaginative invitation to the circle:

Take yourself back into the flow of your childhood. Call up memories of play.

> *Bring your whole self into this re-membering. Body and heart, as much as mind, time, and space. Let images of other beings, human and not, along with feelings, sounds, touch, movement, and smells, wash over you. Childlike ever.*
>
> *Find a few words to capture what it felt like to be lost in the flow of play.*
>
> *Come back to the present. How do your childhood experiences of play still live in you? Are they present, alive, and enlivening in your work as a teacher?*

This opening imagination flows as a source of origin and destination for a meandering contemplation on play. I pick up threads of questions brought from our not-so-distant past, but they are not woven, weft and warp, into a tapestry of form. They instead move like water, opaque and clear, tributaries and confluences, estuaries and blockages, ultimately flowing out to a larger body that holds them all. Play is like a river.

We are at a new threshold moment in the earth's history. Calling up our collective rememberings of play as a child brings us into the flow of imaginative possibilities for our children and our world. Children are hungry to play. It is my hope that this essay offers thoughts about amplifying what we already know and do regarding play in order to help restore play as a creative and health-giving wellspring for children, and ourselves, and the world.

Much is at stake here. As far-reaching as this statement may seem, the future depends upon making sure that children can play, because play brings forth imaginative and creative thinkers. That is why we, as Waldorf teachers, are and need to be righteously fierce, open-minded, and actively seeking ways to support children's play. A world of depleted imagination will lead to a bleak future, as researchers from the Common Worlds Research Collective note in the UNESCO report, "Learning to Become *with* the World: Education for Future Survival."[1]

If our species does not survive the ecological crisis, it will probably be due to our failure to imagine and work out new ways to live with the earth . . . . We will go onwards in a different mode of humanity, or not at all.

—VAL PLUMWOOD, 2007

Kindred Roots: Freeing the Flow

Alone, there isn't much we can do, but if we stand together, there's an immense amount that we can do.

—JOAN ALMON

It is our task to make ourselves more susceptible and capable of learning. This requires unconditional openness and positive anticipation.

—HENNING KÖHLER

Imagine again. Feel into the inner space of children in your care. Open your thinking heart:

*How does it feel
to stand next to your teacher, silent, without words,
to play alone under a table, vigilant and guarding your toys,
to roar into the play of others, drowning out their cries of protest,
to be tethered to creations of the techno-world?*

Imagine:

*How does it feel, dear children, to not know the sweet, freeing, joyful release of play?
And you, dear Teacher, how do you feel when I, as one of many in your care, am Me?*

Play is a liberating experience for the child; it brings them a feeling of well-being and happiness.[2] In healthy, self-directed play a child is attentive, absorbed, and able to persevere in something of their own choosing. They are curious, lively, and energetic. They are able to tolerate mild frustrations. Their breathing is rhythmic; their speech is relaxed. Children move within a continuous flow of actions and care about friends. They show signs of satisfaction after play. In play, children explore and discover. They look for adventures and physical challenges, like in the rough-and-tumble play that mimics the animal world. They seek both motion and protection. Enclosing, enfolding, and building places of shelter and refuge for self and others, human and animal. The baby, the family, the kitten or dog.[3] Research demonstrates that developmentally appropriate play with parents and peers is a singular opportunity to promote the social-emotional, cognitive, language, and self-regulation skills that build executive function and a prosocial brain.[4]

Play has been a pillar of Waldorf early childhood education since its inception. Waldorf teachers are experts on play, as play is understood in a particular way based upon the writings of Rudolf Steiner.[5] We tend to see play as those activities freely chosen and directed by the children that arise from their own intrinsic motivation.[6] We call this *self-directed play*. Out of this understanding, we may certain expectations about play. These expectations may then guide our work. They also might hamper or restrain us. In our classrooms, we have tended to see a clear separation between self-directed play on the one side and the practical work of the teacher, in which children may join, on the other.

Joan Almon, a former Waldorf kindergarten teacher, a pioneering leader in our movement, and a cofounder of the Alliance for Childhood, was early to observe that changes in the social landscape of childhood were affecting play. As Joan saw it, this called for changes in our understanding of play and the practices needed to support it. I never met Joan, but she is my superhero. Over a decade ago, observing the increasing inability in young children to self-initiate and sustain play—even when the opportunity to do so was available— Joan identified the need for adults to learn to act as play facilitators.

Chapter 5: Re-Membering Play

The 2009 publication *Crisis in the Kindergarten* suggests a mixture of a "classroom rich in child-initiated play" and a classroom of "playful learning" as a balanced ideal. If we believe in the importance of play carried by a child's own will and imagination—which I trust we will continue to do—then children need adults to bring appropriate support and create a suitable environment.

As Joan Almon and Edward Miller write in *Crisis in the Kindergarten*, "Exploring the world through play with the active presence of teachers would stand side by side or even *interpenetrate* (my emphasis) with teachers guiding learning with rich, experiential activities."[7]

The report leaves open the question of how to do this.

The Alliance for Childhood is an international coalition of teachers, medical professionals, university professors, child advocates, and parents. Through Almon's work with this organization, an anthroposophical view of play has flowed into a larger, shared public conversation with others equally dedicated to protecting the right of children to play.[8] In the following sections, I share stories of different approaches and solutions that feed children's hunger for play in order to provoke our own thinking and conversations. My own process of exploration and my discoveries about play have taken me far beyond the confines of a Waldorf or Steiner body of knowledge, because I see play as part of our work for the greater social good. Joan's prescient voice rings clear to me in this regard.

Rethinking Constructs of Space, Materials, and Beauty

What can we learn from others not like us who work in spaces and places not like ours? Public play spaces for children offer inspirations for reimagining play in ways that move away from categories of inside/outside, urban/rural, public/private, self-directed/adult-led. The following two stories offer concrete examples of adults fostering playful learning environments that meet the interests and needs of individual children without requiring direct adult interference. These environments dissolve the polarity between self-directed and adult-led play that has tended to be either/or in our perception, thinking, and practice.

It is also important to find a balance between the needs of the group/class and individual children. A major stream coming out of the pandemic—and merging with what came before—is the need, more pressing than ever, to build trust and relationships child by child. Forging the container for a class—which then potentially becomes a vessel for community—happens in the space most intimate and proximate: the child in front of me. This connection then flows out in radiant beams to form the circle of the class. Throughout his writings on play, Steiner is consistent on the point that every child plays differently:

> The unprejudiced observer will observe soon enough that imitation lies at the basis of play. *But every child plays differently.* When one educates the little child before the age of seven, one must discern very carefully. In order to assess the child's play properly, one needs an artistic sense, because *things are different with every child.* The early childhood educator must school his or her observation in order to develop an artistic eye to detect the individual quality of a child's play.[9]

Story One:

A small girl stands outside in the yard of her preschool. This is not a private school on the hill with access to nature but a Head Start program in a community beset by stress and strain. How does it feel to be a child growing up in a place outsiders label as "crumbling"? The play yard is tiny. The girl sees things that are familiar to her—a plastic playhouse and the concrete tricycle path that bisects a scrappy patch of grass. She pauses. Her widening eyes take in new things: cardboard boxes big enough to stand in, bins of chalk, markers, and string. Bits of colored fabric and costumes hang from the fence, fluttering

Chapter 5: Re-Membering Play

in the wind. Other classmates soon join the girl. They all have permission to play. They had been shown the bins. Yet they hang back, unsure of what to do.

A play facilitator picks up some chalk, squats near a long cardboard tunnel, and draws on the cardboard; the girl edges closer. The adult offers a piece of chalk to the child, who picks it up. She tries drawing for herself. Others join her, and a small group starts decorating the cardboard together. Without speaking, the adult picks up tape and popsicle sticks from another bin and tapes the sticks to the side of a small box. A different group of children come over. The little yard soon is alive with children fully engaged in imaginative and creative play alone and in groups. In an end-of-day reflective session, the Head Start teachers report that the children played in entirely new ways. A few bins of material objects and adults integrated into the space, skillful and thoughtful about how and when to guide or intervene, ignited the transformation. A playground for the imagination. Who is the creator?

Story Two:

Have fun and try not to get hurt or hurt anyone else.
—PENNY WILSON'S SINGLE PLAYGROUND RULE

Better a broken bone than a broken spirit.
—LADY ALLEN OF HURTWOOD

Lady Allen of Hurtwood, a woman of royal descent and an urban geographer by training, was interested in how urban spaces are used. She observed how children played in the bombed out rubble and debris of post–WWII neighborhoods. She saw with the eyes of a child, and what she saw—and brought to words as an adult—was beauty, joy, freedom, endless imagination, and connection. Her work led her to design outside environments, and this in turn led her to address the issues of children's rights and children's need for play. She became a major player in UNICEF.

BECOMING AND BELONGING

In London today, there is another woman who has dedicated her life to creating truly inclusive public play spaces. Her name is Penny Wilson. I do not know Penny. I may never meet her, but she has become another one of my superheroes, because she has made me think deeply about risk, inclusion, and building community and connections through play in an urban setting. Indeed, for me, the literal physical environment of what are called "adventure playgrounds" in Europe raises additional questions about the implicit biases we bring to the aesthetics of space. How do our unexamined assumptions about what we view as beautiful—or even appropriate—play environments for children bring judgment instead of open curiosity? That's a topic for later consideration. Let's return to Penny. She had a single driving criteria for the specific location for her open, public play space. "I want a place where children with disabilities—however defined—can come and play with peers and others." Ponder that calling and aspiration for a moment. Superhero indeed.

Story Three:

Harry was a boy who, like every young child on the face of this earth, wanted and needed to play. In the eyes of potential playmates, however, Harry was different; and this difference brought Harry discomfort. Unease, in turn, brought avoidance. In the "adventure playground," Harry stood apart and alone from the other children, with his mother at this side. Harry blessedly had a helper—Penny. Penny is a professional playworker, as they are called in Europe. Her job is to guide children into play of their own choosing. She was there to help Harry. Penny observes, reflects, and connects with families in order to help guide children into play. She did what she saw was needed so that Harry could play with other children. This is what she does for all the children.

Penny knows there is not one way to play. Let's pause for a moment to consider Penny's role and responsibility more fully. Just what is this well-compensated, academically-credentialed profession, dedicated to supporting play for children in ways and in spaces that would rub against the sensibilities of many Americans? The term *playwork* is deliberately oxymoronic. It is a craft filled with paradoxes. Playworkers are aware that in an ideal world they should not need to exist. They manage the spaces for children's play, but this work needs to be as invisible and unobtrusive to the children as possible. The ideal playworker leaves the children free to play by themselves but intervenes in carefully measured ways to support the play process. She is aware of her own playfulness but does not impose it upon the children. She must necessarily be devoted to the children's play, but shun the role of Pied Piper. One of the most basic underpinnings of the craft of the playworker is to understand that the children's play within the boundaries of a play setting should remain unadulterated by external agendas. Good playworkers will have resources available for children—such as painting supplies—but they do not do "activities." Another part of the oxymoronic nature of play facilitation is the need to be present and not present at the same time.

Penny introduced herself to Harry's people. She visited Harry's home. She learned that bright, shiny objects enamored Harry, and so one day Penny invited Harry and his mother to come to the playground again. On this day Penny floated around the space as the magical pocket lady with treasures tucked here and there in the generous folds of her sturdy, practical coat. When Harry arrived with his mother, Penny reached into her pockets and gave Harry a handful of golden baubles. For the next several days Harry and his new friends had a treasure hunt amidst the rubbly space of this urban playground. This happened, as I see it, because the adults—Penny, along with and Harry's mother—both were the bearers of light for the children.

What arises internally for you from these two intimate stories of play? Plastic bins in the play yard? A single rule for outside play? Meeting the children's needs for entering into play on a one-by-one basis in consultation with parents and family? In her recommendations made on behalf of the Alliance for Childhood, Joan Almon encouraged the use of loose parts and play pods, which we saw in the Head Start program and in the European model of "adventure playgrounds." Loose parts are low cost, open-ended materials that children can play with in a multitude of ways. These are things that adults no longer need and that delight children. One finds such materials in dumpsters and recycle bins. Art of Recycle[10] has a list of scrap stores in the United States. Thrift stores, Habitat for Humanity, and resale stores are also good sources. Many programs offer a rhythm or rotation of the materials in the bins. Small storage units called playpods are often used to house the materials, especially for schools or playgrounds serving many children. Open, community -based, "pop up" play days have been effective in building a wider community by bringing more play to more children. Loose parts are, it seems to me, an extension of the "open-ended" toys and play materials in our classrooms. They also offer an expansion of uses for play materials often relegated to "inside play." Adult fear is a major obstacle in meeting the needs of children for adventurous, child-directed play with open-ended materials. Professional playworkers, like those in our two stories, provide a reassuring presence to parents, but they hold back from intervening in the children's play, which is a boon for the children. They step in only if it seems clear that a child is likely to hurt himself or another child. Penny sees herself as wearing a cape of invisibility. Children have freedom, power, and agency. When needed, however, the cape comes off, and the playworker intervenes.

To play is to risk; to risk is to play.
—DIANE ACKERMAN

Children extend their abilities through risky play and learn to master challenging environments. They generally know how far they can go without actually hurting themselves.
—ALLIANCE FOR CHILDHOOD, *CRISIS IN THE KINDERGARTEN*

It is time to rethink risk and see its benefits as well as its difficulties.[11] Facing risk helps children assess the world around them and their place in it. Children love to see how high they can climb on a tree or a jungle gym. Over time they see their abilities grow; they become ever more confident about stretching their boundaries and taking appropriate chances. They also learn about their limits and the consequences of going too far beyond their limits. As they grow older, they apply these lessons in a variety of real life situations.

Risk is not the same as hazard. In the United States we tend to confuse risks and hazards and try to protect children from both. It is important to differentiate between risks that are visible and which children can assess for themselves and hidden hazards. Hazards are objects that children cannot see or be expected to avoid like broken glass on a usually well-tended playground. Risks are those experiences and objects that are out in the open and obvious. Many play injuries are related to broken or poorly designed equipment.

If you are a child with Tourette's syndrome, you may not be able to abide by the "no-swearing" rule, however much you might wish to. Because Penny's play environment was so inclusive, she had to think hard about a system of shared understanding. The result was her single rule that allowed for dealing with many different ways of perceiving the world and for dealing with accidental or unwitting hurt, emotional upset, and damage to things that really mattered. The rule was fluid and flexible. There was no line drawn in the sand, so children did not spend much time testing boundaries as they often do with rigid rules. She did not believe that a binary approach worked. To avoid this binary opposition requires the play facilitator to be subtle. An example of this returns us to the story Joan Almon relates in the epigraph: two boys stood on a table and each declared himself king. By the quiet suggestion that two kings could co-exist, the boys redirected their budding conflict into play.

Let the Puppies Play: Unpacking "Rough and Tumble":

A rambunctious pack of puppies roll around on the rug. The pleasingly pink round rug that is, in the eyes of Teacher, the circle rug. The puppies see it differently, not that they are seeing or hearing anything at this point. Friends. Bodies. Touching! Teacher's voice slowly and steadily increases in volume. Teacher finds herself repeating herself as she says again to the puppies, "We do not play that way inside." In a weary follow-up statement, again falling on deaf ears, Teacher tells the children that they need to "wait until we are outside."

Expecting children to wait to move their bodies. Preventing children from expressing their inner drive to touch, pounce, wriggle and roll like puppies. Restricting physical play to a single space at a predetermined time in a daily rhythm, typically outdoors. Why? Do tight parameters around rough and tumble play recognize children's needs and who the children are? A commitment to supporting child-directed play is an act of deep respect for the children, their play experiences, and their development. At the same time, it is physical play that is most likely to provoke emotional responses, ranging anywhere from discomfort and unease to fear of chaos and seeming anarchy, from caregivers.

Take a step back from the tussling puppies in the kindergarten to recall the very first physical play experiences of a young child. Physical play begins with a child exploring their bodies, playing with hands and feet, and establishing relationships to another through touch, care, and love. This play is crucial for building self-confidence and loving relationships with other human beings. It is part of the development of movement, physical skills, and the mastery of the limbs. It promotes the feeling of well-being, of being at home in the body. Physical play builds and refines the social brain. It is the most fundamental form of play and the truest expression of what it means to be a child.

The social play of all young mammals is what we call rough-and-tumble play or big body play. This kind of play is an essential part of healthy development. Rough-and-tumble play in the early years provides a wealth of healthy sensory experiences. As chapter 4 on the senses describes in detail, the importance of healthy Foundational Senses cannot be overemphasized. Comfort in one's body and peacefulness in mind and heart are prerequisites for a healthy social and emotional life. Children come to this comfort through movement, like rough-and-tumble play, which metamorphoses into healthy social senses. The more we open up the conditions of possibility for more children to participate in rough and tumble, the more likely our environment is to help children develop trust, tolerance, compassion, and a sense of justice and equanimity in social encounters. Physical play, now prescribed by pediatricians, also develops overall physical fitness, reducing rates of obesity and improving bone and cardiovascular healthy. Children strengthen their sensory awareness through this kind of play and learn how to regulate their strength. They practice self-control. Big body play invites flexible, creative, and social behavior.[12] Animal pups deprived of physical interaction show withdrawn, antisocial, and aggressive behavior. Based upon his research on the absence of childhood play and antisocial behavior in adulthood, the American psychiatrist Stuart Brown believes this kind of spontaneous play is a powerful and positive force for the good.[13]

The National Institute of Health recently referenced the growing body of evidence highlighting the benefits of rough-and-tumble play. Quantitative findings show that in order to successfully engage in rough and tumble play, children must practice perceptual, motor, and social skills. More relevant to the discussion here is the point that this kind of play is also often misunderstood or misperceived. More significantly, researchers note that physical play remains one of the most challenging activities to support in early childhood education and care institutions. What? Why? People may think of physical play in the classroom as complete chaos, with children knocking each other over, but this is not the case. Much of the play labeled "rough-and-tumble" is neither rough nor does it involve tumbling. Current research sees a bias inherent in the term; *full body play* and *big body play* are increasingly being used instead.

BECOMING AND BELONGING

In a study from kindergartens and preschools in Norway, researchers observed that this kind of play includes most play using the full body, including body contact with another individual, body contact with objects, striking objects with feet, hands, or an object such as a stick.[14] Play spanned a wide range of social interactions: chasing games, big body play with and without physical contact between players, and play fighting. This study explored what would happen when children in early care settings had free access to spaces that afforded physically active play, such as rough and tumble.

The findings from the study are many, and merit attention. For one thing, this research supported previous research that shows boys are more likely than girls to engage in full body play across cultures. The study also shows that, in a Norwegian context, caregivers restrict physical play much less outside than inside. However—and this is a big however—children perceive indoor spaces for physical play to be more attractive than outdoor environments. Furthermore, in a physically and culturally supportive environment for physical play, girls participated more fully. The study also observes that boys and girls use the physical environment in different ways. Boys participated more than girls in all categories of rough-and-tumble, especially play fighting. Girls seem to be attracted to less physically demanding (competitive) categories of rough-and-tumble, such as big body play with and without physical contact with others. Most of the play occurred in gender-separated playgroups, although the children often played simultaneously within the same space.

Since the literature shows that participation in full body play is closely connected to children's social skill development, this study advises that early care settings provide safe but challenging environments for both boys and girls. Strategies for supporting rough-and-tumble play indoors included a designated play space in a large, soft floor area with pillows or cushions, small group size, and adult supervision as helpful measures. In addition, these areas should be uninterrupted by nonparticipating peers and free from learning activities. How buildings are designed and how rooms are organized with furniture and play materials affect children's possibilities to make independent choices for free action. This study encourages educators to develop the pedagogical skills to facilitate challenging and safe environments for appropriate indoor physical play. Let all the puppies play.

The Confluence of Storytelling and Story-acting: Connection, Community, and Belonging

> *When you tell someone your story,*
> *that person enters the story*
> *and becomes your friend.*
>
> —VIVIAN PALEY

Human morality...

depends on the interest one man takes in another,

upon the capability to see into the other man....

Those who have the gift of understanding other human beings will receive from this nderstanding the impulses for a social life imbued with true morality.[15]

—RUDOLF STEINER

What do I play?

Who are my friends? Do I have friends? I am feeling really alone. Am I alone?

In recent years we have re-examined what is truly essential for Waldorf early childhood education. The oral tradition of the language arts—storytelling, rhyming, poetry, and song—certainly rises to center stage. Sparking a love for the delicious tones and cadence of language, nourishing inner soul forces, planting seeds for the imagination, easing the stress of a transition, holding mirrors and opening windows. The human voice telling a tale, in whatever form, is a rich living presence in our classrooms. The children are blessed to receive this gift. How might we extend this gift into the realm of play? How might we use storytelling—something that we already are doing—to help build children's imaginative muscle for play in general? How can we use dramatic play to build empathic imitation in order to bring the distinctive persona of individual child into "the group" in friendship, in creative kindness, in trust and acceptance? Is this not the ultimate purpose of play? I share with you another one of my superheroes: Vivian Paley. I want more people to know about her, because I think her body of research-informed work allows us to see our work in a new light. Paley illuminates for us how children come to build social and empathic imitation, emotional and social literacy, connection and community through a confluence of storytelling and story-acting. She also offers concrete and practical steps for expanding upon a practice already in place in our classrooms—our rich craft of oral storytelling.

> *Storytelling is still the only activity I know of, besides play itself, that is immediately understood and desired by every child over the age of two.*
>
> —VIVIAN PALEY

Vivian Paley is described as being as much an artist as a teacher, creative and playful to the end of her life. She was a preschool and kindergarten teacher for over thirty years, a researcher, and author of many books that capture her strengths as a keen observer and listener of young children. At the age of sixty, while teaching at the University of Chicago Laboratory School, she received a MacArthur "Genius Award" for her particular teaching approach to storytelling and dramatic play with children. The approach is deceptively simple. Children are invited to share a story with their teacher. The story may be only a few words, even a single word. The teacher acts as a scribe and writes down the story. The class then acts out these stories. Children share and act out of freedom. A clear rhythm and process brings form. As an anthropologist of her own classroom community, Paley discovered that this teacher-facilitated, co-creative art allowed children to join a complex and diverse social world with their individual identities intact. As she describes throughout her writings, this approach brought belonging for all. The children are happiest, she found, when every individual in the group establishes an identity. In her words, "one role is as good as another, so long as you can be inside the story and become necessary for the group."[16]

Dramatic play is the perfect stage for the theatre of feelings to find expression. When children give each other roles to play, they are able to learn through, with, and in relationship to the other and their experiences. Playing out the dramas resting on their own hearts can be a journey of understanding for children—about their own feelings and about those of others. In the acting out of stories from peers, children recreate themselves in the mood of the other person, reproducing every gesture, facial expression, tone of voice, effecting a "magical transmission of emotion."[17] Empathic imitation in play helps counteract alienation and enhances social awareness. Living imaginatively into the experiences of the other awakens the ability to read the thoughts and feelings of others. As the ancient sages said, the need to know how someone else feels is the rock upon which the moral universe depends. The Steiner-informed book by Sally Jenkinson, *Genius of Play*, uses the voice of "everychild" to convey what is meant by empathic imitation:

> Sometimes I am afraid, sometimes I don't know what to do. Sometimes I am angry. I don't know what the script is, but let me be you.
>
> I want to know how you feel, think and act. I want to know what responsibility feels like, although I can't sustain it. I want to look through the looking glass into your world in the only way I can, through my play. Please help me.[18]

At a time when we see children who cannot imitate—even when surrounded by teachers bringing living examples of meaningful, practical work—it becomes imperative for adults to do more in order to activate other avenues for imitative expression. Sara Smilansky, an Israeli researcher who has studied play in Israel and the United States since the 1960s, found that *sociodramatic play* was an accurate indicator of social competence.

Smilansky identifies eight compelling reasons to support sociodramatic play:[19]

> I must have the appropriate behavior for my role. I need to grasp the essence of a play situation. Playing to a given theme teaches concentration; participation in sociodramatic play requires children to discipline their actions to fit in with the narrative and the roles they have assumed; others may change the story line. This asks me to be flexible. Role-playing offers different perspectives on, for example, how "father" acts. The child moves toward abstract thought and symbolism. Children skilled in dramatic play understand different interpretations and roles and different definitions of various situations and themes, both in school and in a wider context.[20]

Supporting children's storytelling in this way, and to these ends, requires listening, scaffolding, and a willingness to experiment with new forms and practices. Teachers listening to children, children listening to their classmates, and children listening to adults all in the service of better understanding each other—and enjoying each other's stories. Listening extends beyond the immediate circle of the classroom. The Boston public schools adopted Paley's approach as a formal foundation of its early childhood curriculum. Their experiences with its implementation may help guide our thinking. For example, we know we want and need to expand and strengthen our community relationships. The Boston schools explored how to use storytelling to engage families in ways that benefitted family, school, and the children. All flourishing is mutual.

Expanding inclusion into the realm of storytellers brings more than diversity of story as a window into cultural differences. Children hear different narrative styles as well. Tone, pacing, cadence, and gesture also come into the storytelling space as well. Volunteers, older students, or administrators might be recruited to act as the story scribes. Sharing children's stories at conferences with parents/families delights everyone, Boston teachers found, and provides the opportunity to talk about storytelling and how families can support children's learning through stories. For children reluctant to tell stories at school, teachers found that stories sent from home via email or written on paper are a nurturing support.

As we see the need to meet the children on an individual basis, sitting with a child to listen and scribe a story engages children one on one with an intentional and joyful activity. For children learning English, with developing verbal skills, or with special needs, this approach allows teachers and peers to help co-construct stories. Eli, for example, was a child new to the country. English was foreign to him as well. After several months of listening to classmates tell stories and quietly watching other classroom activities, Eli came to the table to tell his story. It was a one-word story: "Eli." Choosing to be the actor for his story, Eli took the stage. As the teacher read his name, he jumped into the air. It seemed this was Eli's way of announcing that he had arrived. Subsequently, he became an enthusiastic participant in classroom activities.[21] Other educators note that this teacher-facilitated practice allowed children on the autism spectrum to enter into play that transferred into blocks and then into other types of play. Teachers have found it helpful in practicing self-regulation skills like waiting, taking turns, and deferring. Others note an increase in creative ideas and imaginative thinking. How does one tell a meaningful one-word story? How does one act out a flower?

Children live in a violent world. Children are also exposed to violent images through the media. Grappling with issues of power and control, many children are drawn to stories involving superheroes and fighting. These have long been features of children's play and stories.[22] Whether or not to censor stories with violent themes is a controversial issue. Teachers have to make decisions about how to respond to children's stories that contain violence. Many teachers are uncomfortable with allowing stories with fighting and violence even while understanding that stories are a way children make sense of the world. Paley argued that in helping children safely dramatize these stories, teachers help children learn that they control the story, not the other way around.

Our Playfulness as Wisdom and Practice: Cultivating a Ludic Mood in Life

> *The opposite of play is not work.*
> *It is depression.*
>
> —BRIAN SUTTON-SMITH

"The Essentials of Waldorf Early Childhood Education" by Susan Howard (appendix I) notes humor, joy, and wonder as qualities that we want to be present and living not just in our classrooms but also in *ourselves*. Humor shares a root with humility and humanity and humus. That common root is Earth. I find this connection curious and a compelling gateway to thinking about how adult qualities of humor and humility relate to a playful mood for the classroom and set a model of imitation needed by many children. I am drawn to this word, *ludic*, which simply means playful. Holding a ludic mood of self may, I suggest, bring us closer in attunement to children hungry for play—and closer to families and colleagues in a spirit of joy and connection. The world needs that.

Ponder for a moment a person of wisdom and humility. How does their humility express itself? Everyone needs superheroes of lightness.

Fred Rogers, the creator of *Mister Rogers' Neighborhood*, lives for me as such a person. In spirit and soul he embodied a fusion of great gravitas and playfulness for untold millions of children for over thirty years. He choreographed the production of each show in a meticulous

Chapter 5: Re-Membering Play

and exacting manner. Every word scripted, every song self-composed and flowing forth in the moment with seeming spontaneity and certain joy, curiosity, and playfulness. Mister Rogers was as gentle and loving in real life as on screen, but he also had an iron will and perfectionistic standards. He believed in—and worked every day to emulate—a divine being (Jesus for him) who welcomes children, loves us just the way we are, and calls us to love ourselves and our neighbors.[23]

The film archives of his productions capture the subtle, layered nuances of these qualities, just as they also reveal a person always gentle and sometimes awkward. His lightheartedness is not pie-in-the-face comedy. Extrovert he was not. The content and style of his teaching on social and emotional skills contain things relevant to adults today. As I consider what a world with artificial intelligence will mean for today's children, I also turn to Fred Rogers as an icon of hope in his revolutionary transformation of the medium of television as a force for good.[24]

How does it affect you when you witness lightheartedness between two people? How does it move you emotionally to recall, for instance, Michelle and Barack Obama making merry on stage together? Shared smiles and gentle banter floated through a space otherwise confined to and defined by politics and power. What? A playful president and first lady stepping out with humility on behalf of humanity! Is that not an antidote for the political polarization we now bear witness to? Or consider the relationship between the Dalai Lama and Archbishop Desmond Tutu. The intimacy of that relationship never fails to lighten and inspire me. See the reciprocity of intimate touch as one cradles the face of the other, crinkled smiles on both.[25] Listen to how each speaks in turn with profundity and sanctity interrupted by literal giggles. Humor brings them together. Levity becomes sustenance. Despite separate biographies of long suffering, humility forms the ground for a forward-looking hope.

"It is much better when there's not too much seriousness," said the Dalai Lama. Rudolf Steiner discovered some truth in that for himself when, in his twenties, he learned to play. In order to meet the needs of an individual student's development, he gave himself that assignment. He did this with great satisfaction, as he said himself.[26] Really.

> *If we preserve all through life a mood of being able to learn from life...*
>
> *not simply accumulating knowledge*
>
> *but growing inwardly better and richer*
>
> *—then we have gathered wisdom.*
>
> —RUDOLF STEINER

Plato wrote that you discover more about a person in an hour of play than in a year of conversation. Let's move from a relationship between two to a larger scale. How might a ludic mood in teaching and relations help create and cultivate community and bolster its well-being? It seems to me that bringing more playfulness into faculty meetings, for example, or sharing observations of play in daily check-ins brings form and reframing to our striving for positivity and circles us back to the heart of our work: the children.

The whole notion of a ludic mood in teaching and life is predicated on the idea of social relations. Play and playfulness are social by nature. It is this social nature that positively impacts well-being. Providing opportunities for teachers to interact in a playful manner enhances interpersonal connections and all the benefits associated with them. Bringing observations and stories of play from the classroom is one place to start. Research on playfulness in adults shows positive psychological benefits: joy and happiness, along with qualities like flexibility and creativity that are essential for the times.[27]

There is no one way for a person to be playful.[28] Just as we recognize that what is play for one is not play for another, we can hold ourselves with tenderness, openness, and creativity to discover a ludic mood in our work and life. In the kinship structure of the superheroes whose stories I have brought to you here, we see that there are multiple ways to be a person. This bids our own individual light to shine, just as it then shines forth in radiance to each individual child, which in turn radiates back to the parents and family.

Light. And Heart.

> The epigraph by Val Plumwood is from a book review published in *Australian Humanities Review* ("A Review of Deborah Bird Rose's *Reports from a Wild Country*: Ethics for Decolonisation, issue 42, http://australianhumanitiesreview.org/2007/08/01areview-of-deborah-bird-roses-reports-from-a-wildcountry-ethics-for-decolonisation). Joan Almon, quoted in the first epigraph to the section "Kindred Roots," cofounded WECAN in 1983 and cofounded the Alliance for Childhood in 1996. The first epigraph to story two, by Penny Wilson, is from *The Playwork Primer* (Alliance for Childhood, 2010); the second, by Lady Allen of Hurtwood, is from *Memoirs of an Uneducated Lady* (Thames and Hudson, 1975). The first epigraph to story three, by Diane Ackerman, is from *Deep Play* (Vintage Books, 2000). The epigraph by Vivian Paley in the section "The Confluence of Storytelling and Story-Acting" is from *The Boy on the Beach*; Rudolf Steiner's epigraph is from *Man and the World of the Stars* (Anthroposophic Press, 1982). The epigraph by Steiner in the section "Our Playfulness as Wisdom and Practice" is from "The Great Virtues," a lecture given in Zurich, Switzerland on January 31, 1915 (GA 159).

ENDNOTES

1. Common Worlds Research Collective, "Learning to Become *with* the World: Education for Future Survival," UNESCO (November 2020), https://unesdoc.unesco.org/ark:/48223/pf0000374923.

2. Rudolf Steiner, *On the Play of the Child*, edited by Freya Jaffke (Spring Valley, NY: Waldorf Early Childhood Association of North America, 2012), 45.

3. See appendix II.

4. Michael Yogman MD, et al., "The Power of Play: A Pediatric Role in Enhancing Development in Young Children," *Pediatrics* 142, no. 3 (2018), https://doi.org/10.1542/peds.2018-2058; this is a clinical report from the American Academy of Pediatrics.

5. See Steiner, *On the Play of the Child*; and Angelika Wiehl and Wolfgang-M. Auer (eds.), *Understanding Child Development: Rudolf Steiner's Essential Principles for Waldorf Education* (Spring Valley, NY: Waldorf Early Childhood Association of North America, 2020), chapters 4.8 and 5.8.

6. Edward Miller and Joan Almon, *Crisis in the Kindergarten: Why Children Need to Play in School* (College Park, MD: The Alliance for Childhood, 2009).

BECOMING AND BELONGING

7   Miller and Almon, *Crisis in the Kindergarten*, 12f.

8   See, for example, the UN Convention on the Rights of the Child, adopted November 20, 1989, article 31, https://www.ohchr.org/en/instruments-mechanisms/instruments/convention-rights-child; Yogman et al., "The Power of Play"; National Institutes of Health, "It's a Kid's Job," NIH News in Health, accessed February 15, 2024, https://newsinhealth.nih.gov/special-issues/parenting/its-kids-job; and Oluwatosin Akingbulu et al., "Towards a World of Play and Connection, for Every Child," UNICEF for Every Child, June 30, 2022, https://www.unicef.org/blog/towards-world-play-and-connection-every-child.

9   Steiner, *On the Play of the Child*, 43; emphasis mine.

10 See www.artofrecycle.org.

11 Joan Almon, *Adventure—The Value of Risk in Children's Play* (CreateSpace, 2013).

12 J. Panksepp, *Affective Neuroscience: The Foundations of Human and Animal Emotions* (New York: Oxford University Press, 1998).

13 Stuart Brown, *Play: How It Shapes the Brain, Opens the Imagination, and Invigorates the Soul* (New York: Avery, 2009).

14 Rune Storli, "Children's Rough-and-Tumble Play in a Supportive Early Childhood Education and Care Environment," *International Journal of Environmental Research and Public Health* 18, no. 19 (2021):10469, https://doi.org/10.3390/ijerph181910469.

15 Rudolf Steiner, *Man and the World of the Stars: The Spiritual Communion of Mankind* (New York: Anthroposophic Press, 1982), 52.

16 Vivian Gussey Paley, *The Boy on the Beach: Building Community Through Play* (Chicaco: University of Chicago Press, 2010), 132.

17 Daniel Goleman, *Emotional Intelligence: Why it Can Matter More than IQ* (London: Bloomsbury Publishing, 1996), 115.

18 Sally Jenkinson, *The Genius of Play: Celebrating the Spirit of Childhood* (Gloucestershire, UK: Hawthorn Press, 2001), chapter 3: "Teaching the Heart," 897.

19 Edgar Klugman and Sara Smilansky, *Children's Play and Learning: Perspective and Policy Implications* (New York: Teachers College Press, 1990), 25.

20 Edgar Klugman and Sara Smilansky, *Children's Play and Learning: Perspective and Policy Implications* (New York: Teachers College Press, 1990), 25.

21 As in Ben Mardell, "Boston Listens: Vivian Paley's Storytelling/Story Acting in an Urban School District," *New England Reading Association Journal* 49, no. 1 (2013): 60.

22 See, for example, Vivian Gussey Paley and Susan Engel, *Boys and Girls: Superheroes in the Doll Corner* (Chicago: University of Chicago Press, 2014 [1984]), and Evely Goodenough Pitcher, and Ernst Prelinger, *Children Tell Stories: An Analysis of Fantasy* (New York: International Universities Press, 1963).

Chapter 5: Re-Membering Play

23 See, for example, Shea Tuttle, *Exactly as You Are: The Life and Faith of Mister Rogers* (Grand Rapids, MI: William B. Eerdmans Publishing, 2019) and Michael G. Long, *Peaceful Neighbor: Discovering the Countercultural Mister Rogers* (Louisville, KY: Westminster John Knox Press, 2015).

24 I recommend the Fred Rogers Institute in Latrobe, Pennsylvania. This also is a helpful source for a wide range of research on early childhood development, including play. The Educators' Neighborhood includes links to episodes with certain themes, such as trust, anger, communication, family, and so on (accessed February 15, 2024, https://www.fredrogersinstitute.org/educators-neighborhood).

25 See video from the film *MISSION: JOY*, directed by Louie Psihoyos, at Mission: Joy, https://www.youtube.com/@MISSIONJOYFILM; see also Doug Abrams, Desmond Tutu, and the Dalai Lama, *The Book of Joy: Lasting Happiness in a Changing World* (New York: Avery, 2016).

26 See Wiehl and Auer, *Understanding Child Development*, 170.

27 René Proyer and Willibald Ruch, "The Virtuousness of Adult Playfulness: The Relation of Playfulness with Strengths of Character," *Psychology of Well-Being: Theory, Research and Practice* 1, art. 4 (2011), https://doi.org/10.1186/2211-1522-1-4.

28 For a thought-provoking and fuller discussion of "more than one way," go to Pedagogy of Play, a research collaboration between the LEGO Foundation and Project Zero, which formed out of the Harvard Graduate School of Education. The project includes multinational research sites in Denmark, South Africa, Colombia, and the United States. I found it very helpful in its cross-cultural indicators of playful learning and playful educators: https://pz.harvard.edu/projects/pedagogy-of-play (accessed February 15, 2024).

BECOMING AND BELONGING

6:
The Healing Power of Social Games
Ruth Ker

One day, out on the playground, Jeffrey was looking up at the clouds while I swept the walkway beside him. "Look!" he said, pointing his finger up at the sky. "Do you see that? My grandma is dancing with the angels again."

A few days later, Jeffrey was playing inside with some friends. They had been playing "rescue" over and over again during the preceding days. This involved one child laying down with their eyes closed and others coming to minister to them by calling out, wrapping them in silks, pretending to give them food and water, and so on. The patient either did not survive or was miraculously healed. It seemed to depend on the child's whim as to whether the healing would work on any particular day.

One day Jeffrey took out one of the classroom planks and, very insistently asking his friends for their help, lay down on the plank with his eyes closed. The children were then instructed to carry him around the room. After this had happened several times and both teachers were enlisted to help, Jeffrey quickly got up, put the plank away and went off to play somewhere else.

Introduction

As we have read in chapter 5, the profound benefits of self-directed play and its ability to help the child digest life events have a strong impact on the health and well-being of the developing child. Jeffrey's Mom and Dad were working parents, and his grandmother, being his daily caregiver during the weekdays, was a loving and strong presence in his life. It was a shock to all of us when we heard that Jeffrey's grandma passed suddenly one spring afternoon. He was away from school for a few days while he and his family attended celebrations for his grandma. During this time, Jeffrey had seen his grandmother as she lay in the coffin, and he had also witnessed the processional carrying of her out of the funeral home.

When Jeffrey came back to school, he joined into the play with his usual enthusiasm. He worked through his experiences of his grandmother's death in various ways, and in particular in the events described above. This is just one example of the healing power of self-directed play. Jeffrey, through play, was processing life in a way that was understandable to him. In this case, I did not need to orchestrate a way to help Jeffrey deal with his loss. My role was to provide a place where he could safely play out these scenarios. This is how he made this major event in his young life digestible for himself.

In addition to self-directed play, there are also opportunities in the early childhood environment for the caregiver to endorse this vital activity of play by supporting it at times when we gather the class together. How can we bring the healing power of play into our circle times, outdoor activities, and transitions? Playing games as a group is a compelling way for children to bring their authentic selves to an activity that supports their social-emotional well-being. Whereas circle time can often be met with resistance from some children, playing games is almost always embraced with enthusiasm and joy. Games can also be a healing balm for habits that some children have adopted in response to the trauma of our times.

While many games have a healing influence on the young child because of their content, the actual act of playing games, the exchange of joyful interactions, is also healing in itself. Almost any game that an educator loves and brings with joy and goodwill will have pedagogically healing qualities for the individual child and the group.

The Gesture of the Adult's Presence

In an article published at Anthromedics, the gesture of the adult's presence in the child's life is emphasized.[1] Social games are an opportunity to practice healing gestures in a form that naturally beckons the interest of the children. Something magical happens in an early childhood program when the educator, who has the interest of the children, dons the cloak of playful lightheartedness during group times. Playing games with the children provides closeness and safety, demonstrates socially appropriate ways of being, strengthens a sense of justice, and offers examples of self-regulation. And, perhaps most importantly, these games help children build relationships with one another as well as reconnect to their own vital forces and sense of well-being.

Rudolf Steiner expresses one of the values of game-playing in this way: "It is very interesting to draw attention to the fact that, what we possess as faculties for our intellect, for our experiencing life, for our social times, all this we owe to our early years of childhood, when the games are properly directed."[2]

Playing games in a safe environment can also help remedy stress-oriented behaviors like the fear of being in a group, shutting down and numbing out behaviors, the inability to share, and the fear of losing control. The structure of the game is consistent and predictable and allows the child to begin to trust the "way of the game." The game provides a safe space for the child to practice and build self-confidence.

Engaging in meaningful play through games can also contribute to the child's capacity to self-regulate, to practice opportunities to sometimes be in control and sometimes not, and to trust that interacting with others in playful ways can be safe and fulfilling. For children who are having difficulty playing with others, these games can be strong motivation to help them gain flexibility and spontaneity, relax their containment and/or fear of interacting, and make new strides in their willingness to enter free play.

Playing games can also be a way that the educator can strengthen the bond between themselves and the child. When a caregiver becomes enthused about "playing" a game, they are speaking the child's unspoken language. At the same time, the caregiver is reinforcing the connection that the developmental psychologist Gordon Neufeld mentions in his work on attachment, letting the child know that you are there for them. This is explained in more detail in chapter 9, "The Healing Deed." The child can feel that playing with others in this scenario is safe and that there are dependable parameters. The caregiver personifies the inner gesture, "I am your person, I am here for you," for the child without having to express it in words.

Summary and Suggestions

In summary, we know that young children tend to explore and relate to their world through play. However, childhood trauma can cause children to numb out, shut down, and develop adaptive behavior that separates them from others. When children engage in group games that are carefully led by a trusted adult exhibiting joyful, playful energy, a kindred resonance can begin to happen. An unspoken language begins to develop between the adult and the children in the group. This can be a valuable asset for the child who is building the courage and stamina to enter play with others. Skills can be built in this safe harbor of playing games.

Introducing a wide range of traditional games, fingerplays, and songs from around the world can help harmonize the social atmosphere of the class. WECAN also publishes a comprehensive list of books that have been published to aid the early childhood practitioner in developing their circles, games, and group imaginations with the young child.

Below, I have listed some of my favorite healing games to play. The games referred to can be found in the book *Please, Can We Play Games? Joyful Interactions with Young Children*.[3] I have listed the page numbers of the games for your convenience, but the book is full of child-centered games submitted by early childhood practitioners from Canada and the United States. You may find others that appeal to you more. Here are a few of my suggestions:

(1) In games about animals, modeling ways an animal can self-soothe can provide a way for the children to calm themselves down and therefore set a calmer tone for the group game. Perhaps the pony is nervous about getting new shoes. "Let's stroke the pony gently. He likes to be touched softly on his legs and his belly. My pony likes to be rubbed right here. Where does your pony like to be petted?"

A little later, the children can stroke each other gently too. This can be a way to gently minister to touch-sensitive children who are afraid of the touch of others or to encourage the children to self-regulate their own touch. Sometimes the educator needs to be close to certain children when this happens.

> *Pitter, patter polt*
> *Shoe a little colt*
> *Here a nail, there a nail*
> *Pitter, patter polt*

(2) Games that emphasize taking turns, where everyone is included, and that give others a chance, like "Here's a Pretty Branch So Gay" (75) and "Oats, Peas, Beans and Barley Grow" (73).

The educator can also organize the game so that children who have expressed an unconscious bias toward another child or adult can be paired with that person to swing together in the movement dance. Of course, this must not seem to be obvious but rather a natural outcome of the game. Games like this can be healing for the social dynamic in the class and helpful for creating a land where everyone is welcome.

(3) We can play our way into helping the children control their own impulses by providing games where they could easily lose control, but, of course, in order to participate in the spirit of the game, the child must decide to self-regulate. Often, when the children are given free rein to "gallop" or "fly" outside the circle, those with impulse control issues will demonstrate an inability to rein in their own movement. However, gradually, maybe not at first, their desire to be part of the game can be stronger than their impulsive side and they begin to imitate the way their friends play the game. "We Have Some Little Ponies" (20) is a helpful game that can assist with these possibilities. The educator might say something like, "I'm pretty sure the animals come right back to the barn when the farmer calls them."

Or, while playing "My Pigeon House" (74), the teacher could say, "The birds want to come back to the nest. I'm sure they don't fly up into the castle."

(4) Sensory games can be tremendously helpful in desensitizing sensory issues, especially if repeated over time and if the child is given the freedom to enter at their own pace. Much is gained by these children when the activity is slowed down and they can sense into it when it is administered to others. Then a child who has touch, vestibular, proprioceptive, and other sense challenges can eventually gain the courage to come forward into the game. It's particularly important for

Chapter 6: The Healing Power of Social Games

the educator to set the child up for success at this point. Helpful games include "The Sandwich" (44); "All Around the Sandwich Shop" (45); "Rockabye Baby" (45); "Caterpillar Roll" (45); and one of my favorites, "Little Brown Bulb" (22).

These are just a few of the healing games that I have had the pleasure to play with the children in my care. The educator's relationship with the children and their relationships with one another transforms in the alchemy of these joyful interactions. Including games in our early childhood programming is definitely one way we can create healing environments for the children of the world.

ENDNOTES

1   Rolf Heine, "Nursing Gestures in Early Childhood Nursing, Therapy and Education," Anthromedics, September 25, 2018, https://www.anthromedics.org/PRA-0615-EN.

2   Rudolf Steiner, *Understanding Young Children* (Silver Spring, MD: Waldorf Kindergarten Association of North America, 1994), 54.

3   Ruth Ker, *Please, Can We Play Games? Joyful Interactions with Young Children* (Spring Valley, NY: Waldorf Early Childhood Association of North America, 2018).

BECOMING AND BELONGING

7:
"Here I Am!" Positive Identity Development for Every Child

Leslie Wetzonis-Woolverton

1968: When my family moved to an affluent neighborhood outside of Washington, DC, we were the first Black/African American family to move into that all-white, exclusive neighborhood. It was a brave decision for my parents to make. They anticipated and understood the difficulties everyone, especially their two children, would face. The majority of neighbors and their families accepted us. A few felt we did not belong there. Earlier, I had seen three little girls close to my age playing outside in their nicely manicured yard. As the moving trucks were being unpacked, I raced toward their house in hopes of making some new friends.

When they saw me, the three girls exchanged startled glances, laughed, and shooed me away like strong winds blowing leaves. Turning away in tears, I ran back home as fast as I could to the arms of my mother and father. Although I was crushed, my parents sat down with me. My mother, cupping my chin gently in her hand, told me that I was beautiful, loved, and born with an open heart for all. Embraced by my mother's wisdom and my father's patience, I believed them when they told me that I was not ugly, not unworthy, and would be able to fit in. The most important wisdom they offered that day was to stay true to myself.

BECOMING AND BELONGING

That is my first memory of not being included or belonging. I was three years old, and that memory is as clear today as it was then. With a huge backyard, I turned to nature and my family for protection and solace. I did make great friends (friends I still hold dear today) with other children in the neighborhood, but I was aware that I was different from the other children at my school. From that time forward, I would heed my parents' advice and did my best not to label or judge people in any way—by color, ethnicity, religion, socioeconomic status, nationality, ability, or gender, but to see their inner qualities and meet them first as individuals.

As I grew older, their words would continue to guide me in my life. And now that I am a mother of a beautiful son in his twenties, I know the strength it took from my mother to hold onto the picture she had for me and my brother behind her veiled pain. With tears in her eyes, she and my father had no choice but to use words to try to explain the deeds of others or the unjust reality of the times to someone so young. Although both of my parents are gone now, their voices of love and encouragement continue to ring strongly in my life.

Each of us comes into this world with our unique gifts and dreams. Yet when we are not valued or seen, these gifts can become lost treasures that are never recovered. Our sense of self emerges from the sum of our memories and lived experiences starting with our earliest memories, even before we take our first steps. Repressed childhood memories will often surface in adulthood. How we view ourselves through the eyes of others can strengthen or diminish our emerging sense of self. This is especially true for young children. And is even more the case for children of color, children from other religions, children with special needs and abilities, and children questioning traditional gender labels.

In the book *Weathering: The Extraordinary Stress of Ordinary Life in an Unjust Society,* author Dr. Arline T. Geronimus explains the harmful health effects of social injustice on Black, Brown, and Indigenous peoples (BIPOC, Black, Indigenous, and people of color). *Weathering,* as Dr. Geronimus's research shows, begins in childhood and carries through into adulthood, resulting in shortened life expectancies for BIPOC people. Her research documents how the effects of not being valued, seen, or heard in positive ways harm the health of individuals in nondominant societies. This reality has also been confirmed out of my work as a WECAN Co-coordinator of Inclusion, Diversity, Equity, and Access. Out of the many stories that have been shared with us, we are beginning to understand the impact that social inequities have on becoming and belonging.[1]

> *2023: I was visiting an early childhood class at the beginning of the school year and witnessed a five-year-old boy collapse into his mother's arms as she was speaking to him privately in the administrator's office. He was crying that he did not belong and was not wanted. He hated his size, his skin color, and everything about himself. No one wanted to play with him or be his friend. His mother told him that she loved him, that all of his family loved him, and that he did have friends. They hugged each other, but the little boy continued to sob and held tightly onto his mother.*
>
> *Passionately, his mother reassured him of her love and still, he needed more. He needed affirmation from others, from his teacher and classmates. He recognized me from earlier visits and hugged me tightly after he began to feel more collected. In that moment, the three of us moved from tears to joy. His mother took my hand, for we both understood what was needed in that moment. I reached for his hand and suggested that we go back into the classroom together. The two of us stood tall and walked into class. Every day during my visit, I would meet him outside of his classroom, and we would walk hand in hand to class, smiling and confident. With the support of being seen, loved, and valued, he was able to begin making new friends, and in time he emerged as a leader in the class.*

Diversity and Inclusion Begins with Us

Learning how to support all of the children in our Waldorf classrooms begins with us. Cultivating an interest in others and deepening our understanding of belonging and inclusion always begins with us as individuals. There is no other way. To meet each other in today's vast world of differences, we must discern what lives in our hearts that is arising out of conscious or unconscious stereotypes, biases, assumptions, and judgments.

Our inner work is necessary for us to learn how to dissolve bias and all forms of discrimination in relation to individuals and humanity as a whole. It takes daily inner striving to bring new eyes so we can experience one another with appreciation and gratitude. This work of loving ourselves and each other, of true acceptance, can blossom into small successes in our classrooms and, in time, to significant societal shifts in our worldwide garden.

I will say it again. The work must begin with each of us! You can start by exploring the relationship between identity and acceptance. Sit with your eyes closed and imagine what the opposite of belonging and positive identity might feel like for nondominant cultures and ethnicities, even under the umbrella of good intentions. Consider why we use the word *other* to identify people in matters of inclusion and belonging. Where are you with the social questions of our day? How does technology promote stereotypes and contribute to the othering of the world today? Adolescents are bombarded with ideal images that result from an old vision that excludes far too many. What are our new pictures of beauty? Can you tell stories that don't offer only masculine pronoun (or stereotypically gendered pronouns) but remain open? We need to be aware of and begin to understand the eight social (socially constructed) identifiers: race, ethnicity, sexual orientation, gender identity, ability, religion/spirituality, nationality, and socioeconomic status.

Check in with yourself about the content you want to share with your class. If it feels uncomfortable in any way, research the history of the culture from which you are sharing and make sure you are bringing a true picture and not a stereotype. Keep the eight social identifiers in mind as a guide. Question assumptions that you might be carrying toward a group or groups of individuals. What are our expectations for boys? What are our expectations for girls? What thoughts do you carry around gender bias? Is it right to expect minority groups to assimilate? What do you know about the true histories of the Native American and Indigenous peoples? What do we know about discrimination based on socioeconomic status? Why are religions so entangled in judgment of others when their stated goals are to love and seek light?

We need to explore our unconscious biases of yesterday, today, and tomorrow. We need to bring honest questions into our work with children, families, and colleagues. Do we find ourselves open to differences or do we label children and families quickly? Can we unpack what we carry that may be implicit bias? *Implicit bias* can be defined as a mental process that stimulates negative attitudes about people who are not members of one's own "group."

With implicit bias, the individual may be unaware that their biases, rather than the facts of a situation, are driving actions and decisions. Implicit bias involves subconscious feelings, perceptions, attitudes, and stereotypes that have developed as a result of prior influences and imprints. It is an automatic positive or negative preference for a group based on one's subconscious thoughts. Implicit bias does not require animus; it only requires exposure to a stereotype to produce discriminatory actions that have effects on nondominant groups. Implicit bias can be just as problematic as explicit bias because both may produce discriminatory behavior that can be harmful.

Rudolf Steiner and the First Waldorf School: An Excerpt from *The Spiritual Ground of Education*

The following excerpt reminds us that, beginning with the founding of the first school, Waldorf Schools were intended to be inclusive:

BECOMING AND BELONGING

The Waldorf School was founded in Stuttgart by Emil Molt from the midst of the emotions and impulses of the years 1918 and 1919, after the end of the war. It was founded, in the first place, as a social act. One saw that there was not much to be done with adults as far as social life was concerned; they came to an understanding for a few weeks in the middle of Europe after the end of the war. After that, they fell back on the views of their respective classes. So, the idea arose of doing something for the next generation. And since it happened that Emil Molt was an industrialist in Stuttgart, we had no need to go from house to house canvassing for children, we received the children of the workers in his factory. Thus, at the beginning, the children we received from Molt's factory—about 150 of them—were essentially proletarian children. These 150 children were supplemented by almost all the anthroposophical children in Stuttgart and the neighborhood; so that we had something like 200 children to work with at the beginning.

This situation brought it about that the school was practically speaking a school for all classes (Einheitschule). For we had a foundation of proletarian children, and the anthroposophical children were mostly not proletarian, but from the lowest to the highest. Thus any distinctions of class or status were ruled out in the Waldorf School by its very social composition. And the aim throughout has been, and will continue to be, solely to take into account what is universally human. In the Waldorf School what is considered is the educational principles and no difference is made in their application between a child of the proletariat and a child of the ex-Kaiser—supposing it to have sought entry into the school. Only pedagogic and didactic principles count, and will continue to count. Thus from the very first, the Waldorf School was conceived as a general school.[2]

In this first Waldorf school, the goal of the education was to bring peace after so much divisiveness during World War II. In our times, we also need to address the cultural divisiveness with as much light and peace as we can create. Our children are asking for this. Our young people are asking for this. The imagination that has always inspired me is of a full "world garden" in which all of humanity is represented.

Becoming a Loving Advocate

In addition to uncovering and working to dissolve our own biases, there are ways we can work both inwardly and outwardly with the children in our classes, especially those who seem to need extra support. This work starts with observing and listening to every child with an open heart. Imagine how it feels to be a child who is always questioning whether or not they will be accepted. Can we take the child and their family into our sleep with wonder instead of judgment? Can we ask for insights and guidance from our spiritual helpers? Can we communicate with clarity, compassion, and understanding? Can we respond with interest, creativity, and resilience?

Other ways that we can support individual children include:

- Taking time to develop a personal relationship with every child
- Cultivating a deep interest in the family through home visits and checking in regularly
- Taking the child by the hand, walking and talking with the child
- Creating opportunities to do work tasks with the child or a small group of children
- Setting up games in a way for the child to be a key part of the group
- Structuring conversation at snack to consciously include the child in a positive way

BECOMING AND BELONGING

- Creating therapeutic stories for the child
- Demonstrating care for the child to the other children through all of the above
- Affirming to the child that you are there for them through all of the above

It takes time to develop a personal relationship with all of the children in our class. It requires cultivating an interest in our class children and families that is not superficial. Regular check-ins with parents can keep problems from arising. Sometimes, consulting with teaching colleagues for their observations can be illuminating. Home visits done at the start of the school year can give the teachers important information. When outdoors, walking and talking with children one-on-one can offer the child welcome attention and may allow new insights to arise. Taking the child by the hand for a one-on-one moment can enhance trust. The love we share with the children in our care goes beyond sympathy and antipathy.

Creating opportunities to do work tasks with the child or a small group of two or three children is helpful to many children. When big and small feelings occur, address the moment right away and include the child who has been unkind. The teacher can sit with both children, one on either side. In these moments of stillness, equanimity can arise and empower the children better than any moralizing. We need to be present and model positive intentions toward the possibility of healing. This allows both children to move freely into a future space together, leaving "what just happened" behind.

Simple games in which everyone can become a part of the group again can also help heal moments of distress for individual children. In my class, I always cultivated snack-time conversations in which the teachers consciously modeled and guided positive contributions. Snack times and story time provide opportunities for therapeutic stories that can support and heal social issues occurring in your classroom. It is important to keep these stories general and try not to isolate a specific child's behavior.

Demonstrating your care for an individual child to the other children through all of the above activities assures all children that you are there for them all. Your care must always be authentic and come out of real interest. A positive sense of belonging shapes us all. In becoming an advocate, we are learning to work from our hearts. It is hard work, but it provides a space for us to meet one another in the fullness of our humanity in everything we do. The pressure for assimilation is removed when we are allowed to grow and flourish as our true selves.

Other Ways to Embrace Children and Their Families

In Waldorf early childhood education, during the first seven years, young children need to experience that the "world is good." For me, the world for the young child should also be beautiful and trustworthy. How we meet the young children entrusted to us is extremely important. Just as important is cultivating an intentional community that is respectful of parents and families. Our work in inclusion and belonging is supported by the stories we share, the festivals we cultivate, and the seasonal circles we create. All of these activities also support the children's experience of goodness.

Fairy tales and storytelling are crucial components in supporting cultural belonging. Through exploring tales from many cultures, we can build a fuller world picture to share in our classrooms. I recently discovered a beautiful Middle Eastern tale that showcases the human capacity for kindness. *The Camel in the Sun* by Ondaatje Griffin is a universal tale of kindness and empathy.

We also want to continue to explore the question, "What pictures am I bringing to young children?" Many of us can recall a story from our childhoods in which someone was excluded or othered. Through thoughtful reflections on these stories, new clarity can shine into our memories. Acceptance can become the solid ground underneath our often walked paths. Can we let go of social hierarchies stemming from past circumstances? Can we let go of stereotypes? When we begin the work of facing uncomfortable truths, we can begin moving toward a future that honors us all.

The stories and fairytales we gather should arise out of our real interest in order to be authentic to us and the children. By appreciating the universal imaginations from world sources, as well as keeping well-known stories, we are adding to the body of work from which we can draw inspiration. And by seeking new stories and tales from other cultures, we stay open to renewal in our work. I am also inspired by newly created stories that address current issues of our times.

Celebrating diversity even when none is visible in a community is another essential step in this work. For example, read the story of "Sweet Porridge" by the Brothers Grimm. How will you bring this story to the children? What racial identities will your puppets have? If you have Black, Indigenous or people of color represented, which characters are they? By switching the puppets so different racial identities represent different characters, the teacher can illuminate poverty as a state that could be experienced by anyone or offer a different perspective on where power resides. I have consciously reversed roles in telling this fairy tale and only the adults noticed the change to the traditional picture.

The Work Goes On

In my twenty years of teaching, I brought a world that includes us all to the children in my classes. The work I did then and continue to do with new teachers is learning to see and value the gifts in all people. Becoming a vessel of grace is work for us all. We are not born with hate or othering. This is learned behavior. Our work now is to honor, reimagine, and leave behind the stereotypes and dissolve the "other" label. It is always important to remember that each of us has a story

Chapter 7: "Here I Am" Positive Identity Development for Every Child

or stories to tell. May our stories and journeys lead the way to kindness, love, and strength. For kindness and love is never weak! There is so much in this work that we must do together to transform our vision into a lived reality.

We can expand our work with the children by initiating conversations with parents, grade school colleagues, faculty, administrators, and boards. These conversations should never be brought with a sense of dismissiveness or judgment. The essence of our work toward inclusion, diversity, equity, and access is to create bridges by listening deeply. This is hard work. Sometimes it is painful work. If it is done out of love, it is also delightful work. If the sense of identity of one child is impacted positively, then the heart of humanity is enriched. Wounds and conflicts in the social world in which we are embedded will begin to heal. The journey is ongoing. It will take being present one day at a time, one year at a time, one decade at a time. The difficult moments should not be avoided, but embraced with curiosity and open hearts.

Some additional questions to explore:

- How do you meet the "difficult" parent, colleague, and child?
- How do you look at yourself when you are feeling reactive? Are you living in sympathy and/or antipathy? How do you cultivate empathy and enkindle true interest and trust?
- If there is resistance to this work, what is at the root of the resistance?
- How do you incorporate these concepts in parent evenings to build bridges toward a more inclusive, equitable, and kinder community?
- How can I self-audit my classroom and my interactions with parents, children, and colleagues?

By adopting culturally responsive antibias approaches to all the social identifiers in parent and school-wide communications, this work will

BECOMING AND BELONGING

begin to be much more natural in your classroom work. Review the literature you plan to share with families in your schools, *especially* in school communities without diversity. What does an example of a parent letter to families include that has culturally responsive information? How do we share our interest and encouragement with class families and colleagues in order to build real interest in belonging and inclusion? How do we actively listen in openness when disagreements occur?

Below, I share with you a short, written meditation from a book I have carried with me for most of my life. It supported my picture of love and hope for an inclusive society. The title is *The Awakened Heart: Meditations on Finding Harmony in a Changing World* by John Robbins and Ann Mortifee from the Inner Light series.[3]

Social Action as the Way of Love[4]

A mass of fear has been passed on from generation to generation, sapping our strength and causing us to mistrust and do violence to one another and ourselves. It can be seen not only in war but also in the preoccupation with war that leads nations to arm themselves against one another and drain the planet of precious resources.

But at the same time, there is something life-affirming and eternal that is always with us. There is love, there is a web of light and healing that is spun around this troubled Earth. If we are to make peace in our world, our families, our professions, and our lives, we must activate our healing powers by choosing love over fear.

It is tempting to become so absorbed in external problems that we lose touch with our inner peace. If we want our lives to be a vehicle for the kind of world for which we pray, we need to keep our hearts open, even when we take a stand in protest. We may disagree most fervently, but we need never become hardened.

When the heart shuts down, we isolate ourselves from the world. When we protest our fear, we bring as our message not more harmony but fear. And we suffer from the very disease that we seek to cure.

If we wish to strengthen our beautiful and wounded world, we must take a stand on behalf of all humanity. Then we express the kind of power that has been represented by such people as Martin Luther King, Jr., and Mahatma Gandhi. They stood for, spoke for, and lived for peace. They saw the darkness, they saw what must change for the human spirit to take its next step, but their protest was not based in fear. They were willing to go to jail if need be, to suffer, to be treated with cruelty, but they knew they had to live with their hearts open, or they would only add to the burden of hatred and violence already active in the world.

We need never let our aversion to what others are doing get in the way of our love and acceptance of them. When we are no longer against anyone but are taking a stand for all, then we become truly effective peacemakers. Our life becomes a statement that the real enemy is the fear that clouds the human heart and not the person who is acting out that fear.

Fifty Years Later—A Story Is Born

With their cloak of love, my parents always supported and embraced me and my hopeful view of the world. I was given the "talk" that many parents of color give to their children at the age when my trust in the world was still forming. In my heart I still clung to hope. Knowing who I am today allows me to listen to the birds, seek walks in nature, sit underneath trees, and return to the feeling that I remember as a child—of love, safety, joy, and soulful breathing. Below is a story I wrote during a summer storytelling course that I co-taught some years before work on this book began. It is about my first experience of not belonging (being othered). It is a story that offers healing and hope. May it serve to deepen your understanding of our collective work!

Let's continue to listen to one another and actively try to find a balance between sympathy and antipathy in our work of inclusion, diversity, equity, and access. Remember, the path of self-discovery is essentially heart work. I, too, am still on the journey and this work will be lifelong.

The Story of Grandmama Enisi's Quilt

Lina had thought over and over what her father had said to her on the first day they arrived in their new home. Lina was three, excited for the big move away from her familiar neighborhood. Yet Lina could not stop thinking about those girls. Just yesterday, she had found girls her own age, three sisters, she would find out later. They would not play with her. Why did they laugh so loudly as she walked away? Why could they never imagine playing with her?

Their voices in unison, "We do not play with brown Barbies or you!" Because she was brown, these words would follow her for years. Echoing in odd moments, she would be surprised when they surfaced, so determined, again and again, demanding her to go away, to leave. The words from her father, full of wisdom and comfort, made sense, "Keep trying for friendship, never to give up seeking friendship from all people, and stay in joy."

But Lina could not help wondering why being brown, pink, white or purple made any difference. Lina now wanted to go back home to where there were more children her color, to her first home that she had left. She told her parents over and over before falling asleep. This place was too different. It was unwelcoming and unfriendly. On their front door was a sign in cursive writing, which she would learn later, spelled their family's name, followed by, "Welcome All."

Lina's grandmother had come to help their family unpack and would stay with the family through summer. As soon as Lina leapt from her bed that next morning, after tossing and turning most of the night, she immediately sought her grandmother's love and assurance.

"Come and see me outside, Lovey."

Lovey was Lina's nickname given to her by her grandmother. Ladybug was her nickname from her mother and father. Although there had been so much unpacking to do, Lina's grandmother was sitting outside in the sun on a chaise lounge. Rest before work, she would say now, having worked so hard all of her life.

Lina silently witnessed the grace and peace her grandmother had always shown as she lifted her head to the sun, taking in the warmth as the sun moved through the day. Her grandmother always did this specifically at this time of the year.

"Summer's beginnings," she would say. "Summer is still gentle and new."

The move had been quick, the packing fast. Their old backyard had been nice and homey, but this backyard was green and expansive. Frances, which was Lina's grandmother's name, could hear the birds singing clearly overhead, the tall grass in need of cutting, blowing softly with the wind. The noise of honking traffic was long gone, left behind in their old neighborhood.

This move had placed her family in a peaceful Chevy Chase suburb without sirens, car horns, or occasional loud shouts from passersby and neighbors. Frances felt at peace. Still, she was aware that they were the first "Negro" family to move into this all-white neighborhood. Frances was extremely proud of her son, a successful young doctor. Her son, now an up-and-coming psychiatrist, was well on his way. The struggles and sacrifice that allowed the family to move to their new home were worth it. It was the best decision and outcome of her son's lifetime of study and hard work. Yet . . .

Frances had unpacked the quilt she had been hand stitching since Lina was born, placing her sewing basket by her side on the blue, worn flagstone. Smoothing the quilt out, Frances smiled, knowing that once completed, this quilt would be Lina's, just like the quilt she had made for each grandchild before. It was draped over her legs when she first heard Lina come outside with the bang of the screen door. It was a sound she loved to hear in the first warm days of summer, no matter where she lived.

"Lina, my dear, what is your hurry? Come give Grandmama Enisi a big hug."

Lina was in a hurry. Her heart was still heavy. She needed to run.

Lina listened to her grandmother and gave her a huge hug. She fingered the faded floral, calico fabric of soft ocean blues and cornflowers. Lina's head was cast down as she focused on the intricately hand-stitched flowered squares.

Frances could tell there was something wrong. Lina was an extremely happy child. She was always talking about the world of her stuffed animals, her beloved dolls, and the wonders of nature. She would talk about her big brother too, but it was usually about how he would break into her tea parties, disrupting her stuffed animals and dolls, sometimes running off with her toys—the usual big brother stuff. This morning, Lina's exuberant joy was missing.

"How did you sleep in your brand-new room last night, my Lina? The stars were golden, so big and bright. The moon stayed awake the whole time, never sleeping, for she and the rabbit talked all through the night."

Lina looked up from her fingering. Grandmama always told her that at certain times, the moon and the rabbit, embraced in a golden circle, talked with each other. Her grandmother's ancestors had filled her full of stories when she was small. Lina's large tears immediately fell.

"Grandmama Enisi, I saw three girls yesterday playing in their yard. I wanted to play with them, and they said, 'No.' I did not have any Barbies to play with them with. When I went home to get mine, they said they did not play with brown Barbies or me, because I too was brown. They said they did not know me, did not want to know me. I kept telling them I was Lina. My family had just moved here, a few houses away. They laughed, pointed at me, and went on with their play! They kept saying, 'No, go away.' They said that I would never be someone they would ever want to play with!" Lina scrunched up her face tight just as they had.

Chapter 7: "Here I Am" Positive Identity Development for Every Child

Frances moved the quilt aside and cradled Lina in her arms, humming a familiar song she sang to her granddaughter and grandson when they both were sad. She sang this song gently, the way she learned it from her mother when she was a little girl. Lina continued to cry, and Frances patted and rocked her. For Lina, this was a known embrace, full of her grandmother's blossomy scent and, in the quiet shushing, there was comfort, hope, love, and acceptance.

"Daddy told me that there are good and not-so-good people. That I should continue to try and make friends, but if they still are mean and unfriendly, it is their loss. To not say what they said to me about me to others I will meet now and later when I grow up and become big. What does color even mean? Brown, white—I just wanted to play." Lina's soft cries had turned into sobs.

"Lina, my dear, please listen to the birds above, flying in the sun. They are red, black and brown, and blue. They fly together high into the sky and land together amongst the branches that are also different."

Lina paused her crying and looked up high toward the branches and over the lush green tall grass. She could hear the birds' soft calls, their different songs as they flew free or perched safely on the high branches.

Frances continued, "The butterflies and bees land on all the flowers in the meadow. They do not wait to see what color of nectar comes from each type of flower, but they seek the sweet nectar from every different flower they land on."

Lina's cries softened and she blotted her eyes. This was true.

"Grandmama Enisi, why are your squares different shapes, different colors, and different sizes?" Lina had begun to finger the worn and evenly stitched fabric again.

"For the very reason as I just told you about the birds, the butterflies, the flowers, and the bees. Everything wants to be seen, appreciated, and loved for who and what they are. All living things are different—people, animals, and everything in nature, right down to each blade of grass, each star in the sky, you, my dear, your grandmama, Enisi, and the fabric in this quilt. I select each square and I think of the world. Your daddy was right in what he told you." Frances smiled as she held her granddaughter firmly and gently at the same time.

"It will take time to understand these things, Lina. Yet, I hope it will not take a lifetime. I place different pieces of fabric one shape at a time. That is how life is for us, also."

Frances saw that Lina had begun to lose interest in their conversation, and her tears were now dry. And with a new inquisitive focus on a ladybug resting on a lavender floral square, Lina hopped off her grandmother's lap.

"Look Grandmama Enisi, a ladybug!" Lina said. She quieted down, thinking, and said, "I think I understand. I am going to go play now."

Lina kissed her grandmother on her cheek and went off to follow the ladybug as it sought real flowers to land on. Lina hummed the familiar song that her grandmother had hummed earlier. She would believe her grandmother's explanation of how the world should be. The wisdom of those words, her mother's grace, and her father's advice would last her full lifetime. Years later, when she was the same age that her brother was then, she would experience this heartbreak again and witness her mother's beauty and strength addressing ignorance about race. But for now, Lina laughed and giggled, darting and dancing as she followed her new insect friend.

Frances knew her granddaughter would be fine ... in time. At least as fine as a young girl of color could be in this world that would see her skin before her heart. Life is a mountain to climb. Enisi could still hear the very words of her own grandmother, who taught her about the world as a little girl. These conversations must be shared. The question is always when. This decision to move was not made lightly. Her son and daughter-in-law talked for hours about what would be best. Lina's brother would also face rejection. He was six years older, still a child, but as a young black male in the post–civil rights era, a threat to nice white society.

Together, as a whole family, they would wait and see if any friendships would be formed with the little girls only a few houses away. Whether it happens or not, life's real quilt—full of joys, heartaches, and always open to love—will shape her granddaughter's life in ways not yet determined.

"Yes, indeed," Frances said out loud to her quilt, "Rabbit and moon were in full conversation last night!"

> *Have enough courage to love.*
>
> —MAYA ANGELOU

The ending epigraph appeared at @DrMayaAngelou, the poet's official social media feed at twitter.com, November 1, 2013. She is also widely credited with the inspiration to "Trust love one more time, one more time, and always one more time."

ADDITIONAL RESOURCES

Brothers Grimm. "Sweet Porridge." Story 103 in *The Complete Grimm's Fairy Tales*. New York: Random House, 1980.

Griffin, Ondaatje. *The Camel in the Sun*. Toronto: Groundwood Books / House of Anansi Press, 2013.

Harris, Nadine Burke. *The Deepest Well: Healing the Long-Term Effects of Childhood Trauma and Adversity*. Boston: Mariner, 2021.

ENDNOTES

1. Arline T. Geronimus, *Weathering: The Extraordinary Stress of Ordinary Life in an Unjust Society* (New York: Little, Brown Spark, 2023).

2. Rudolf Steiner, "The Organization of the Waldorf School," chapter 7 in *The Spiritual Ground of Education*, (n.p.: Anthroposophical Publishing Company, 1947), 90.

3. John Robbins and Ann Mortifee, "Social Action as the Way of Love," in *The Awakened Heart: Meditations on Finding Harmony in a Changing World*, part of the Inner Light series (Tiburon, CA: H. J. Kramer, 1997).

4. Ibid., 106. Reprinted here with the author's permission.

8:
Face to Face, Heart to Heart, and Full of Imagination!

Speech as the Living Bridge between the Emerging Self and the World

Holly Koteen-Soulé

Grandma, her grandson, and his father were sitting in the living room. The boy, who was four years old at the time, seeing his father glance down at his lit-up phone, said in a surprisingly authoritative voice, "Put down your phone, Dad!" The implication was clear: I am talking to you. His father complied, of course. Grandma smiled inwardly.

Five years later, the scene was similar, but this time, the boy was engrossed in his iPad. Dad, a little frustrated, raised his voice a bit and said for the second time, "Son, I'm talking to you." Grandma smiled inwardly. Her secret hope was that none of us would lose our capacity or appreciation for the incredible gift of human conversation.

A child's first words bring incredible delight to both child and parent or caregiver. It is similar to the jubilant sense of achievement at the child's first steps, but also different. Lakshmi Prasanna, in a lecture to early childhood educators, described the differences in these two milestones in a helpful way. In standing and walking the child experiences, for the first time, distance between itself and the earth, between itself and others. This sudden sense of separation creates a longing to fill the space with speaking. Both experiences, separateness achieved in walking and reconnection achieved in speaking are necessary initial steps in the child's developing capacity for human encounter.[1]

The process of learning to communicate through language, however, has been prepared not only through movement development, but also by the quality of a child's preverbal interactions with the humans in their world. The impulse of the child's social-emotional life begins before birth with the child's responsiveness to the sound of the human voice. Some mothers sing or speak to the child during pregnancy and have noted the special responsiveness of the baby in utero or after birth when those same songs or words are repeated.

The Evocative Power of the Human Voice

Singing to our babies is, more often than not, their introduction to the sound of the human voice. The sound of singing accompanied by rocking calms and soothes the fussy infant or baby that is struggling to fall asleep. When a child is able to sit comfortably in an adult lap, traditional songs and nursery rhymes give them much joy. In these instances, it is not the meaning of the words that matter, but the melodic and rhythmic qualities of the speech to which the children respond. What the child takes in is the feeling tone and the qualitative aspects of the language. We are preparing the ear and the heart for the myriad of differentiated social-emotional experiences they will have in the world, as well as the different kinds of beings with whom they will have relationships.

A human voice can thunder or whisper, wail or whine, shout or sing. It can moan or caress, simper or cajole! The list of possibilities is nearly endless. What are the possible responses to those voices? The thunder could be experienced as inspiring or frightening. Cajoling could be experienced as manipulative or encouraging. The baby and young child take in every aspect of their environment, not only the tone of the speaking, but also the conscious or unconscious intentions of the speaker. For those of us who work with young children, it might be helpful for us to try to remember the significant voices in our own childhood and how we were affected by the sound of those voices. The power of these experiences for the young child come from the clear undertone of emotion in our speaking. The child withdraws or is drawn to the emotional tone of the communication. What kinds of sounds or quality of voice invite a child into connection and relationship? How might these early experiences affect the child's future social-emotional development?

The Foundational Senses Prepare the Soil of the Soul

We have already noted how important standing and walking are to the subsequent acquisition of speech by the young child. Walking, as the significant milestone of the child's first year, is the result of the healthy development of the senses of self-movement and balance. As explained in greater detail in chapter 4, the foundational senses metamorphose into the spiritual or social senses. The sense of physical balance is intimately connected with the sense of hearing and our capacity to listen, while the healthy sense of self-movement prepares us to perceive the movement shapes and forms of language and the ability to communicate with another human being.

The senses of touch and life are the primary in the life of the infant and are equally critical to the child's unfolding social capacities. Through touch, the infant senses a boundary and has many experiences of "not I," which over time firm up the child's sense of "me-ness" on this side of the boundary. The child's touch experiences come in many varieties- firmly reassuring, gently calming or delightfully stimulating! Warm, loving touch by a fully present caregiver nurtures the budding sense of relationship. The child responds, non-verbally at first, and the archetypal pattern of "speaking" and "listening" is established.

The potency of touch is beautifully expressed in a short passage from Jacques Lusseyran's memoir *And There Was Light*. Lusseyran had an accident and became blind at the age of eight. In passage below, he speaks about touch as a doorway to a deeper kind of understanding. While we understand that touch gives the child the sense of "not I," it can also invite the child into loving relationship, leading ultimately to the capacity to sense the "I" of the other.

> If my fingers pressed the roundness of an apple, each one with a different weight, very soon I could not tell whether it was the apple or my fingers which were heavy. I didn't even know whether I was touching It, or it was touching me. As I became a part of the apple, the apple became a part of me. And that was how I came to understand the existence of things.[2]

The sense of touch and the sense of life go together. The way we care for a child's bodily needs is significant. Careless or matter-of-fact caregiving is a missed opportunity for social learning. Presence and interest in being with the child during feeding, bathing, dressing, and so on invites the child into relationship. Children for whom loving care is modeled will have the chance to imitate the same kind of care with the objects and people in their environment. Building the capacity for relationship starts from the beginning of life and is nurtured by how the humans in the child's environment care for and interact with the child, even before the advent of speech. The discovery of the existence of mirror neurons by infant researchers has confirmed our understanding that infants as young as a few weeks old learn foundational social-emotional skills, such as how to communicate, express needs, and share emotions from interacting with their caregivers.

In the book *Beginning Well*, the authors point out the qualities that they regard as most critical to building a trusting relationship with a child. These qualities are acceptance, respect, empathetic care, authenticity, and certainty.[3] To my mind, the importance of these qualities is not limited to the first year of life and can be emphatically ascribed to all of early childhood and beyond as qualities that support the development of social-emotional capacities.

Living Language: Supporting the Transition from Nonverbal to Verbal Communication

When a child is nonverbal, parents, teachers, and caregivers need to practice sensitive observation of a child's moods and behaviors. We learn in time how to read the needs and wishes that are expressed nonverbally. This is a kind of listening that is actually deeper than the way in which we might listen to someone's words, and it is how we can best support the very youngest children. We may respond to the nonverbal child with smiles, singing, words, or actions. Our responsiveness is the critical aspect that strengthens the child's future capacity for healthy communication. The child reciprocates, at first without words, but with a clear understanding of the efficacy and joy of human dialogue.

When the child is ready to speak, we can support them with clear and simple speech. Single words connected to concrete objects or activities are most readily accrued. We must, however, refrain from "baby talk," and give them well-formed language to imitate. The explosion of a two-year-old's vocabulary is almost impossible to fully appreciate. The three-year-old loves to hear simple stories about everyday activities. Children from three to five years of age are nourished by repetitive and rhythmic stories that include poems and songs. The older children are ready for more imaginative stories and fairy tales. These stories bring to life the rich palette of feelings and emotions, allowing the child to "try on" those emotions in preparation for meeting them more fully later in life.

For young children, everything in the world is alive, has a soul, and speaks to them! The more we can speak in picture images, the more we can affirm the living power of language. Rie Seo wrote a wonderful article in *Gateways* newsletter about how she rediscovered imaginative language as a key to supporting the children in her kindergarten. In her article she reminds us that the child's relationship to words is different than ours, that "the outer world begins to resound in their souls in pictures. The words are there not to give them information, but to offer experience through sound, movement and imagination."[4]

She advises parents and early childhood teachers to rediscover "soul-language," so that when we speak, we unite our earthly language with qualities, pictures, or archetypes. Imaginative language can conjure up a picture that invites children to step into it with joyful will. She offers some simple examples: "Piggies have to slip into the barn to stay warm." "Old Grumpy stays in the garden." "Robin is resting in her nest."[5]

Disturbances to Speech Development

More than twenty years ago, concerns about how media was affecting the speech development of young children were brought to our attention in a small pamphlet called *Childhood Falls Silent*, published first in Germany and then translated into English by Waldorf colleagues in Australia. The main culprit at that time was the television. Research seemed to indicate that the significant rise in speech disorders came less from medical factors than from changes in sociocultural factors. Researchers concluded that exposure to speech coming from an electronic source deters speech development, while hearing human speech promotes development.[6]

In 2023, the influence of media, not only on the young child, but also on older children and adolescents, has grown exponentially. Every year since then more books are written to warn us about the dangers and to advocate for less media and more real world, human connections. An excellent resource for parents was published in 2019, titled *Growing Up Healthy in a World of Digital Media*.[7]

A more subtle but equally significant concern has to do with adult use of media, especially smartphones, in the presence of children. Being focused on one's phone clearly diminishes the quality of any potential interaction with a child and models a lack of interest in or a real capacity to be truly present to another person. A child will take in the underlying message that a phone is more important than a person. The acceptance of this as normal by the adults in the family will likely have a negative impact on the child's ability to be present in their social interactions.

Too much or too little talking in the child's home can also impact speech development, as can unkind or age-inappropriate speech. Environmental or constitutional difficulties may also impinge on normal development. In the same way that healthy movement is an essential foundation for speech development, healthy speech is necessary for the development of future thinking and academic learning. It is also necessary for healthy social-emotional development, including the capacity for engaging in meaningful communications and enduring relationships.

Speaking and Listening

When a child says, "Water," and a glass of water appears, the child experiences the magic of language. We see both amazement and triumph in the child's reaction. Language is a fundamental and uniquely human capacity. Speaking is not primarily about the transfer of information, but about bringing out and giving form to an impulse that was formerly dormant in the soul. It is a creative activity from the viewpoint of the individual speaker and, because it connects the speaker with the surrounding world and other beings, it is also a socially creative activity.

The physiology involved in the speaking of a word is complicated and involves many fine inner movements. It has been discovered that when we listen to someone speaking, our larynx moves in synchrony with the inner physical movements of the speaker, below the level of our consciousness, of course. This is how the child learns to speak and why the child needs a human voice and not a machine to imitate. These physical movements are the first step of listening. Physical movements in the listener are followed by feelings or soul movements and, finally, by the movements of thoughts when new conceptual understandings arise. "As such speech resounds through the whole person from below upwards and not vice versa."[8]

Children who are learning to speak need time to shape their inner experiences into language. We offer support when we give them time to form the words, without interrupting them or finishing their sentences for them. We offer support when we listen attentively, nod or respond simply, "Hmm." We offer support when we join in their delight in whimsical language. Children of all ages are grateful when they sense we are listening with an open heart to what they have to say. It gives them courage to share what might otherwise stay unsaid. Speaking and listening are skills required for healthy communication and real conversation.

Rudolf Steiner defined conversation as the archetypal human phenomenon. It was his experience that when one is listening, one falls asleep to oneself, and when one is speaking, one wakes up to oneself. In this description there is a kind of natural breathing between the speaker and the listener. The implications of this characterization are profound. When social difficulties emerge, it is more likely than not that the healthy balance between speaking and listening, between the self and others, has been disturbed. Is there a healthy balance in our own lives between speaking and listening?

Working with Conflict and Redeeming Unkind Words

Differences, disagreements, and conflict are a natural part of life. Opportunities to experience and work through conflict, whether it is expressed verbally or nonverbally, is an important aspect of social-emotional learning. Children are often given the message that conflict needs to be avoided at all costs. Alternatively, children may be familiar with conflict, but never experience conflict being consciously resolved. When teachers acknowledge conflict as a part of life that can be worked through so that we can better understand others, it becomes less of a challenge and more of an opportunity to be welcomed. Working through conflict is another way of learning to balance speaking and listening.

Chapter 8: Face-to-Face, Heart-to-Heart and Full of Imagination!

Like other aspects of what we do in the presence of the children, how we regard conflict and manage it in our class will have the strongest influence on the children. With toddlers and sometimes older children who are distraught, we offer support by giving them some starting words. For example: "It seems like . . .", or "You both want to . . .", or "Your friend wants to tell you something." We need to place ourselves close to the children in such a way that invites them both to be fully engaged.

If we want children to learn how to negotiate a resolution, we should not take on the roles of judge and jury or instruct them as to how the situation must be rectified. In the beginning of the year, they may need encouragement and suggestions. For example: "I wonder how you can both . . ."; "What would happen if . . ."; "I have an idea." With practice, they will become adept at coming up with win-win solutions.

While most young children are by nature empathetic, those who are exposed to unkind words and behavior may try them out on others. Children may also repeat statements containing harmful racial, gender, or cultural stereotypes. In these cases, a teacher needs to intervene clearly, compassionately, and creatively. Kindness must surround unkindness without resorting to the need to blame or shame. Asking or requiring a child to say, "I'm sorry," is less meaningful than encouraging a child to find a way to help the one who was hurt feel better. In the same way, a teacher's proper use of *please* and *thank you* is the preferred means of cultivating politeness.

In early childhood we try to provide models of exemplary behavior rather than using rewards or punishments. Our aim is to support the children's capacity to build an inner sense for what is socially appropriate rather than legislating from the outside. Even praise can distract from this aim. Finding words that show interest in what a child has accomplished without evaluating it is sometimes difficult, but well worth the effort because of how it can strengthen a child's sense of self.

Here are some additional ways to elicit cooperation or verbally guide young children. Helpful phrases include: "It is time to...", "Let's all go to...", "You may...". In a situation where it's appropriate to offer a choice, offer two equally acceptable choices. If there is no choice, do not offer or ask, "Do you want to ... ?" When a child needs correcting, it is more effective to say what is expected rather than what should *not* be done. Use your imagination liberally. "Isn't it amazing that eyes come in so many different shapes and colors, but all of them sparkle like the stars?"

Every teacher can be triggered by certain behaviors of individual children or an unusually rowdy tidy-up time. These are opportunities for us to find new capacities for clarity and kindness in our speaking and doing. Meeting these situations, including those that arise with parents and colleagues, with willingness and creativity serves our own social-emotional development as well as that of the children.

Healing through Sounds, Silence, and Speech

Early morning birdsong, wind rustling in the leaves, and water babbling over rocks can fill our souls with peace and harmony. This is one of the reasons that walking in nature can be so restorative. In some places we can offer this daily refreshment to our young children. If we live in a noisy city, it is more difficult. We need to make sure that there is a genuinely quiet pause every day that allows the children to rest and digest the stimulating activity of their lives. This pause can be enhanced with gentle singing, harp playing, or no sound at all. The enduring experience for the children will be the way in which the teachers imbue the space with calm, loving attention.

The quality of our voice is an aspect of the early childhood classroom environment that moves the children deeply. If we sing all day, the children will stop hearing us. We become like the background music in the mall. We know that while the sound of singing "lifts" the children, speaking helps them come "down" into themselves. Moving between singing and speaking provides a naturally harmonizing rhythm. Understanding how tone, volume, warmth, and articulation affect listeners helps us learn how to use our voice more consciously and to become aware of the potentially healing capacity of the human voice.

Our speaking voice can carry a wide variety of qualities, especially if we consciously allow it to resound with the musicality of the language or the images living within what we are sharing. When the language is living in us, then it will also live in and nourish the children. We can give them fresh fare or dried up crusts! Enlivened, picturesque language takes us all on exotic journeys and introduces us to a kaleidoscope of multifaceted experiences that support the child's growing capacity for grasping the range of human emotional life.

Stories and Puppetry as Healing

Human beings are natural storytellers. Storytelling is the way we make sense of our experiences and pass on our collected wisdom from one generation to another. Modern storytelling via the media does not have the same impact as hearing stories in person for the reasons we have already described, and it's more oriented toward entertainment than supporting social-emotional development. Waldorf education honors and utilizes the power of the imagination at all levels, from early childhood through high school and beyond. Nancy Mellon expresses it profoundly in her book *Storytelling and the Imagination*: "Above all, storytelling gives us love and courage for life: in the process of making up a wonderful story, new spirit is born for facing the great adventures of our lives and for giving wise encouragement to others, of any age, along their pathways."[9]

We need to rediscover our hidden capacity for thinking in images, finding images in stories that speak to questions our children are asking, and crafting images into healing stories for our class. Reading and working with traditional stories and fairy tales helps us reawaken to the power of images, symbols, and archetypes. Nancy Mellon advises us to experience symbols as a living part of us. Symbols are connected to the deepest part of our souls, where healing forces are always at work trying to restore balance.[10] When we are deeply connected to the images in a story, whether it is one that we have chosen or one that we have created, our connection to it will enliven the way in which we speak and nourish the developing social-emotional life of our listeners.

With the youngest children, we tell simple stories and typically use puppets to support their growing capacity to connect words and meanings. In early childhood, puppets themselves are often very effective in conveying messages to the class regarding sensitive classroom social situations or addressing an individual child who might have difficulty hearing a particular message directly.

In general, puppets invite us all to step into manifold images of the archetypal human being. A professional puppeteer once shared with me the notion that actors act, but puppets *are*! As such, puppets make every aspect of a story more real. Because of the way that children live inwardly into the embodiment of the puppets, they "move" with them and find great reassurance in the evolution and conclusion of the story. When children move the puppets themselves, they sense, even more strongly, both freedom and agency. Through the conscious use of puppetry, Waldorf teachers can affirm for our children that life is good and that we have both visible and invisible helpers to support us in our development.

Conversation as a Social Imperative

The author of *Reclaiming Conversation: The Power of Talk in the Digital Age*, Sherry Turkle, reports, "Face-to-face conversation is the most human and humanizing thing we do."[11] With regard to children, her warning is clear. Time with media prepares the children for more time with media. Time with people teaches children about relationship, beginning with the ability to have a conversation. What we as a culture are missing from the loss of conversation is practice in the empathetic arts and the experience of community. For Turkle, through conversation we learn how to be vulnerable, feel empathy, and collaborate with others. Interestingly, her research revealed that what also suffers from relationships built on superficial connections and online communications is our capacity to be alone, reflect and know ourselves better.

Knowing ourselves and having an interest in others is at the heart of social life and social development. The lack of face-to-face encounters greatly exacerbates the other challenges to living together harmoniously. Without in-person encounters, our relationships do not have sufficient depth and resilience to help us work through real crises, to grow, heal, and become more whole. We have all had the experience at some time in our lives of having been listened to so deeply that we discovered something about ourselves that had been hidden until it was drawn out by the attentiveness of our conversation partner. Marjorie Spock wrote a little booklet called *The Art of Goethean Conversation*. In it she likens attentive listening to crossing the threshold into the world of living thought.[12]

Conversation is also critical to solving the social questions of our times, including the cultural and social justice issues arising within Waldorf education and society as a whole. We cannot see ourselves or make conscious changes without talking with others whose experiences are different from our own. We need to be in dialogue to recognize our differences and commonalities, learn from one another about our unconscious biases, cultivate compassion and empathy, and learn how to work together to create new solutions and ways of being.

As early childhood educators we need, above all else, to be worthy models for the children in building, tending, and healing human relationships. We need to look at our work in the school and beyond. Questions that we can ask ourselves include:

- How do we nurture a listening mood in ourselves and in our work with the children, families, colleagues, and in the school community?

- How do we foster a culture of conversation in our school community?
- How can we view disagreements or conflict not as something to be avoided but as an invitation to conversation?
- How can we welcome storytelling, cultural sharing, and conversation into our parent meetings?
- How can we model conversation in our classrooms?

Sometimes the healing conversation is wordless—a gesture, a glance, an inner accompaniment. A therapeutic story lives deeply with the children because they connect with the images and gestures as well as the words. We are often "in conversation" without words. In healing, we are in conversation with our bodily elementals. In gardening, we are in conversation with the forces of nature. In doing the backward review of the day before going to sleep, we are in conversation with our spiritual helpers. In a healthy faculty meeting, we are in conversation with the "being" of the school.

In every conversation we have the possibility to meet one another, to meet more of ourselves, and to meet a deeper sense of our humanity. Every human being wants to be seen, heard, and understood. Every heartfelt conversation represents the possibility of meeting those primary needs or providing healing for times when those needs were not met.

A Plea for the Family Meal

When and where do we learn how to engage in meaningful conversations? The long-time tradition of the family meal is becoming more and more rare in North America and possibly in other parts of the world as well. In my parent meetings, I always encouraged families not to abandon this obvious opportunity to practice sharing with one another the many events, joys, and struggles of our daily lives. Without our modeling genuine interest and showing support for one

Chapter 8: Face-to-Face, Heart-to-Heart and Full of Imagination!

another, how can we expect our children to learn basic social-emotional skills? Those social-emotional skills are essential for learning to solve our social issues together, now and in the future.

The more recent idea of conducting "family meetings" can also be useful, but it cannot really replace the social atmosphere that exists when people prepare the meal, serve one another, and share food together. Mealtime conversation has a different quality from a meeting, even though the topics discussed may be similar. At mealtime, there is a natural and wonderful weaving of personal and group concerns, silliness and seriousness, speaking and listening, celebration and problem solving. It is an archetype of our communal existence and our shared humanity. It is, in addition, the perfect opportunity for adults, as well as children, to continue to grow and learn new social-emotional skills.

Kindergarten snack time is the Waldorf counterpart to the family meal and is equally important as an opportunity for social-emotional learning and practice. An absolutely quiet snack does not result in much learning; neither does one in which everyone is talking at once. It is actually an art to create the mood of a family meal, in which we can sense the wholeness of our kindergarten group, while giving space to individual members, and practicing real interest in and conversation with one another. The modeling of conversation between teachers is an essential component of the children's learning. Snack time as an event has an important threefold aspect in which everyone can participate—the preparation, partaking, and tidying away. It is like a daily festival in the classroom that marks the passing of the seasons with gratitude and celebrates the growth of each child and the community as we make our way through the year together.

ADDITIONAL RESOURCES

Faber, A., and E. Mazlish. *How to Talk So Kids Will Listen and Listen So Kinds Will Talk*. New York: Avon Books, 1980.

Heckmann, H. *Loving Care for the Child Under Three*. Oslo: Forlaget Slow Parenting, 2021.

Keihl-Hinrichsen, M. *Why Children Don't Listen*. Edinburgh: Floris Press, 2006.

Kohn, A. *Unconditional Parenting: Moving from Rewards and Punishment to Love and Reason*. New York: Atria Books, 2005.

McAllen, A. *The Listening Ear*. Gloucestershire, UK: Hawthorn Press, 1989.

Udo de Haes, D. *The Singing, Playing Kindergarten*. Spring Valley, NY: Waldorf Early Childhood Association of North America, 2015.

Weber, S., N. Macalaster, and J. Swain. *Singing and Speaking the Child into Life*. Spring Valley, NY: Waldorf Early Childhood Association of North America, 2017.

ENDNOTES:

1. Lakshmi Prasanna, "Speech Development: Giving Birth to Speech," *Gateways* 75 (2018): 6–9.
2. Jacques Lusseyran, *And There Was Light: The Extraordinary Memoir of a Blind Hero of the French Resistance in World War II* (Novato, CA: New World Library, 2014 [1963]), 20–21.
3. Pia Dogl, Elke Maria Rischke, and Ute Strub, *Beginning Well* (Spring Valley, NY: Waldorf Early Childhood Association of North America, 2018), 26.
4. Rie Seo, "Speaking Pictorially," *Gateways* 75 (2018): 14–18.
5. Ibid.
6. Rainer Patzlaff, *Childhood Falls Silent: The Loss of Speech and How We Need to Foster Speech in the Age of the Media* (Australian Association for Rudolf Steiner Early Childhood, 1999), 12–15. This resource was recently reprinted in the Right to Childhood series of booklets under the title *Speech Development in the Digital Age: Hidden Treasures of the Spoken Word* (Spring Valley, NY: Waldorf Early Childhood Association of North America, 2024).
7. Michaela Glöckler et al., eds., *Growing Up Healthy in a World of Digital Media: A Guide for Parents and Caregivers of Children and Adolescents* (Hudson, NY: Waldorf Publications, 2020).
8. Patzlaff, *Childhood Falls Silent*.
9. Nancy Mellon, *Storytelling and the Art of Imagination* (Rockport, MA: Element Books, 1992), 1.
10. Ibid., 177.
11. Sherry Turkle, *Reclaiming Conversation: The Power of Talk in a Digital Age* (New York: Penguin Press, 2015), 1–7.
12. Marjorie Spock, *The Art of Goethean Conversation* (Spring Valley, NY: St. George Publications, 1983), 2.

9:
The Healing Deed
Ruth Ker

One of my mentors used to tell her kindergarten children stories about Jeeves, an imaginary character who delighted in serving others. She found these stories particularly helpful for helping the children model proper manners. One day, it was the turn for a six-year-old to pass around a tray of goodies to the rest of the class at the lunch table. The child with the tray first chose the biggest piece and placed it at his spot before continuing on to serve the others. At that moment the teacher said, matter-of-factly and without judgement, "Jeeves would not have done that." The child went back to his plate, placed the food back on the tray, passed the tray around to the others, and then took the last piece for himself.

As early childhood educators we have the tremendous opportunity to promote healing and also to influence the future healers of the world. This is not an idle ideal. Countless opportunities arise every day in an early childhood classroom where educators can make a difference in the lives of children and their families. The educator is privileged to be present at this formative time in the young child's life and support the youngest members of the next generation—the most recent messengers from the spiritual worlds. These young children are on a devotional path with a mission to discover the meaning of this place and time into which they have incarnated.

Knowing this, we can play a life-affirming part in the young child's developing consciousness and their journey of discovery. By recognizing the profound effect that an understanding word or an empathetic deed can have on a child who is struggling, we can attune to their state of being and accompany them on their incarnational path.

Mantle of Healing

Strategies for child guidance and discipline are important considerations for the early childhood educator. It's helpful to note the root word for "discipline" is "disciple," which means "to follow out of love." When we remember that the children easily sense our inner intentions and see what is imbued by our gestures, we know that "following out of love" is an important foundation of our relationship with all of our children. We want to help children to know that we truly "see" them and are available to address any "discomfort" or "unkindness". This kind of mutuality can build an abiding trust between the child and the adult. The teacher's keen interest, commitment to social justice, and the warm and loving, but not sentimental, soul mood of the teacher is a conduit for the desire to "follow out of love". Freya Jaffke, in her book *Work and Play in Early Childhood,* describes what she calls the "mantle of the classroom."[1] Early childhood educators can create a healing intention that becomes an invisible canopy or a cloak that permeates the entire room. Within this space, we can be a reliable healing presence, awake to what is going on and holding the image of right activity.

One of the important things to realize is that, although there are similar developmental timelines that stream through childhood, each child has their own unique gesture, biography, and relationship to their developmental milestones. An important part of our work is to develop our observational capacity so that, out of actual experience, we begin to notice the unique characteristics of each individual child. The developmental psychologist Gordon Neufeld speaks of the double role of educators and parents. He tells us that we are both angels of comfort and angels of resistance. There are times when the most compassionate and beneficial gesture of the adult is to support the resilience of the child by standing firmly and giving direction in a simple and matter-of-fact way. In this way, the child begins to recognize that there are things that happen that are not acceptable.

On an unconscious level, children give themselves over completely to the serious task of uncovering the mysteries of being in the world. We witness how they drink deeply at the well of those who inspire them. They mirror the activity, subtle gestures, and even the unseen inner responses of those around them, whether those sources of wonder are their parents, siblings, relatives, the family dog, or their teacher. For the child from birth to seven or so, what we do as educators and how we are in our activity is of tremendous interest to them. They definitely place much less interest and are often less able to digest the long abstract explanations we try to bestow upon them.[2]

By refraining from leading the child down the path of intellectuality and instead imbuing our language with living pictures, we are already providing a healing balm that resonates with the child's innate belief in magic. Cultivating this can become a wellspring for imaginative solutions later on in life. Many children in our world suffer from the burden of too much information. Caregivers who have a daily practice of working with living picture imaginations are directly nourishing the child's current consciousness and the possible flexibility of their future creative thought-forms.

What the adult does within the child's environment, how we relate to our work and to others (both children and adults), and the willingness on the part of educators to take an active interest in what needs healing is vitally important for the child's developing sensibilities. Our activity informs these developing "citizens of the world" that it matters how we behave in relationship with other beings and situations. For the educators, paying attention and being present for what is really happening for the young child is the first step that allows us to witness their living questions and consequently temper our own responses according to the child's developmental needs.

The teacher's devotion to the healing deed is in itself restorative. Children want to know that goodness prevails. They want justice and are relieved when there is someone in charge who is committed to assuring that in the classroom, balance will be restored.

Recreating Social Balance

Most of the children who enter our classrooms, sometimes inadvertently, sometimes directly, have experienced situations that have affected their social-emotional responses to life. There is great potential for us, as early childhood caregivers, to build trust and hold a space for healing in the environments we provide. How can we be in relationship with the children, parents, and community so that we support the best possible outcome for these interrelationships? How can we build the child's trust so that they grow in the faith that they live in a world where there is goodness and there are people who know how to do the healing deed?

First and foremost, we must understand the developmental needs of the young child. Children yearn for the world to be a place of goodness. They are devoted to wonder. They need to move, play, and have reliable rhythms to help them self-regulate. They need security, consistency, continuity, and safe limits. They need people and circumstances to imitate. They need to witness the healing deed being regularly enacted in their environment. The far-reaching impact of children witnessing the process of healing is the main message of this chapter.

Early childhood educators have opportunities to provide life-changing environments that affect not only the consciousness of young children, but also their overall well-being. These effects can ripple out into the family and the community and eventually can influence future events in which the growing human being becomes involved. My thoughts turn to Christian, a former kindergarten child, who in grade two showed up at the Kindergarten door one day to tell me something.

He said, "Miss Ruth, guess what I'm going to be for Hallowe'en?"

"Tell me, please!" I said. "I can hardly wait to hear."

He said, "I'm going to be a knight. I'm going to use the sword! You know, the one I made in the kindergarten, the one that brings down the light!"

Two days later, Christian, escorted to the Pumpkin Path celebration by his Dad and dressed in his knight's costume with his sword at his side, was seen holding his sword high in the air again and again; he had spotted a figure in a frightening costume heading in his direction.

As educators, our healing deeds include what we bring into our programming that can be modelled out in the world but, more often than not, the most impactful influence we wield is how we react at the spur of the moment—what we do in situations where individual children are uncomfortable for reasons that are sometimes minor or temporary but, nonetheless, disturbing for them. This has far-reaching consequences, especially if the child is sensitive by nature.

This is a large part of our work that can't be anticipated or included in our daily plan. These situations could be relational, for instance when a child is feeling left out, doesn't understand social rules, or is being treated unkindly by others. It could also be situational, where children come together with different skill sets and are manifesting varied capacities to play, socialize, and self-regulate. In these situations the healing gesture of the teacher—one that brings justice and still helps the children to remain relational with each other—can have significant future effects on the individual and the social fabric of the whole group.

Anxiety can also result from illness, a lack of sleep, or sudden changes in the rhythm of the child's home life. Accompanying the family through these situations and having a willingness to listen and share resources can have a healing effect that connects the home more intimately to the classroom. Eventually, this depth of relationship can contribute to true partnerships with parents and teachers and will have ongoing transformative effects for the child and the family.

Then there are also children who come to us who have experienced deeper trauma, perhaps generational trauma, where the burden of injustices lingers and carries over into family identity and results in cultural and racial reenactment. These wounds are often triggered by many of our unconscious habits. Some further examples are described in chapter 7.

In early childhood, we typically tell pedagogical stories rather than give moral directives, and educators model compassionate behavior rather than insisting on compliance with rules.

However, there are specific instances where we need to stand up in either word or deed for a child or a situation that needs to be clearly identified as needing to be corrected or reframed. A child unwittingly communicating a harmful stereotype to another child or to the group would be an example of such a situation. These opportunities offer educators the chance to model moral courage and are formative for the children and families when the teacher takes hold of these situations with spiritual vigor. Such moments may also present themselves in our work with parents and colleagues.

Ignoring them rends holes in the social fabric of our community.

There are many different ways to support children in distress. Here are some examples: by being physically close; by sharing a comforting gaze, embrace, or word; by being willing to stand for what's just; or by demonstrating empathy and understanding in a picture or a story that serves as a living picture of how we take care of one another. It has been my experience that children yearn for these "wrongs" to be made right, and an unconscious relief often spreads through the classroom when a perceived "wrong" has been righted in some way. Even though some issues cannot be resolved immediately, it still brings the child much comfort to see some form of attention come toward the situation.

Gordon Neufeld, an attachment-based developmental psychologist based in Vancouver, British Columbia, Canada, poignantly describes the primary needs of the young child, "Children need to feel an invitation to exist in our presence, exactly the way they are."[3] This kind of all-inclusive embrace, extended by the adult, is not conditional and there is nothing the child needs to do in order to win our love. The child benefits from feeling that we are their person. We want them, love them, and welcome *all* of them. Gordon Neufeld is repeatedly quoted as saying, "Connect before you redirect." Dr. Neufeld's work builds on attachment and developmental science, and he is able to explain phenomena that are normally difficult to understand, including aggression, shyness, bullying, and counter-will. Dr. Neufeld has many courses for parents and has written a book called *Hold on to Your Kids*.[4]

The repetition of the healing responses we demonstrate for the individual child ripples out into the group and begins to build a community understanding that there is a kind, caring lawfulness that is intrinsic to our time together. As early childhood educators, we have the possibility of building an environment that is a safe and loving place and of giving children the experience that places where we can feel ease and protection do exist in this world. We can be instruments of hope and faith for the growing child!

Understanding Trauma

Sometimes, children who have been exposed to stronger stresses and trauma enter our classrooms. Although we are not therapists, there are still things we can do. Taking interest in the current research around trauma is important. In this article, I am sharing a few of my more recent investigations.

The history of psychology is punctuated with the question of how to heal trauma. Gabor Maté describes trauma by saying, "Trauma is the invisible force that shapes our lives. It shapes the way we live, the way we love and the way we make sense of the world. It is the root of our deepest wounds ... Trauma is not what happens to you. Trauma is what happens inside you, as a result of what happens to you."[5] In his recently published book *The Myth of Normal*, Dr. Maté offers a compassionate guide to health and healing as he looks at the impact of our world on children and the adults in their lives. I definitely recommend this book as excellent reading material for early childhood educators wanting to deepen their understanding of the deep-seated nature of trauma. The word trauma is a strong word that can be off-putting, but if we appreciate that one of its original meanings is "an emotional upset," then we can understand that most children experience varying degrees of this state of being, sometimes on a daily basis.

Peter Levine, a trauma specialist from Colorado, also has helpful advice for caregivers. He encourages us to avoid what most of us usually want to do first, trying to talk the child out of their behavior. The "talking cure" for trauma survivors, he says, is largely ineffective, and practitioners should find ways to help the person deal with the trauma by supporting the person in a different way. He suggests supporting the person, "to give way to the unspoken voice of the silent, but strikingly powerful, bodily expressions as they surface to 'sound off' on behalf of the wisdom of the deeper self."[6] That's a mouthful! Basically, he is telling us to create a safe place for the traumatized person to surface what their being wants to tell us. This is part of the healing. We can deduce what a powerful tool we have as educators—simply allowing the child to invest themselves in creative free play!

Another dynamic that Levine describes is that "when we have been traumatized, we are particularly sensitized to and hyper-aroused by fleeting stimuli."[7] His research makes me think about the puzzling reactions of some of our mystery children when they respond to triggers in their environment in ways that we don't understand; we are puzzled because we don't even perceive that the triggers are there. This sheds new light on working with children to help them self-regulate and have impulse control. Instead of immediately trying to change the child's behavior by "talking them out of it," can we find ways to observe what triggers the child and allow them to manifest this unconscious reaction to life in a safe place? Can we create safer spaces for them until they adjust OR host spaces for the child that help us understand what is happening for the child? Is there a way that we can make it possible for the child to play in unusual ways? Of course, safety needs to be taken into consideration.

I think of Jason, a child survivor of a car crash in which his mother suffered brain trauma. Jason was trapped in the car with his unconscious mother while the rescue team cut them out of the car. His little sister had been thrown out of the car and was rescued more readily. Both children were in the kindergarten together. Whenever the pace accelerated in the kindergarten, Jason would repeatedly respond in the same way. He would drive an up-ended chair around on the rug, at first slowly, and then the speed would accelerate. Then, the car (chair) would topple over and "crash," and it would end up on top of him. For the better part of six months he did this, until one day, he curled up in a ball sobbing. I held him, with all of the warmth and love I could muster. That's all. This happened four times, and after that, Jason rarely went for his "drives." He moved on to other investigations. Speaking to Jason about this behavior was not the appropriate healing deed. Allowing him the space to access what was submerged in his being, to play out the scenario over and over again and to eventually discharge it, was the healing deed.

I would like to share one more quality that the educator can model at times when traumatic reactions surface. Peter Levine also mentions the practice of *pendulation* as a healing tool. Pendulation, also called looping, involves switching between resourcing and/or surfacing the trauma and titration, or pausing. This allows a person to move between a state of arousal triggered by a traumatic event and a state of calm. This helps the body to calm itself and regain homeostasis—a state in which the body's systems are regulated and working in balance.[8] Jason was doing this when he lay for a while on the rug with the chair on top of him. This act of pausing before acting, re-enacting, or reacting to a stimulus is part of the healing journey. For the imitative young child, educators can support healing and the restoration of balance by modeling the simple act of pausing before acting.

Rudolf Steiner repeatedly expresses the ineffectiveness of trying to "reprimand" or "talk children out of their behaviors." We know this is also ineffective in our adult relationships, and yet we seem to be compelled to do this again and again, as if we can "reason" the child out of his behavior.[9]

Our healing deeds may happen in the moment, as mentioned above, or they may be repetitive gestures that occur over a year or more that gradually erode or displace the traumatic experience to which the child is reacting. Eventually, our reactions and responses to individual children can become the child's new way of relating to the past trauma.

The opportunities to provide healing environments for the young child and to do healing deeds are endless, and our attempts to "be the change we want to see in the world" can also be transformative for us. The child, their parents, and the educator are all accompanied by spiritual beings who wait in readiness to help. Sometimes we don't know how to avail ourselves of this support or even trust that it is there, but we can be assured that it is steadfastly present.

In the preparation of this book, the contributors spoke about sharing stories that can give us all hope for the future. In closing, I would like to share Henry's story. It's about the mysterious way in which the spiritual worlds can support us in our work.

Henry's brother was enrolled in my preschool class for two years, and I learned to love and respect his family's loyalty and interest in Waldorf education. Henry used to come to my door in his baby car seat at his brother's drop-off and pick-up time. When I opened the door to receive his older brother, baby Henry would smile broadly, reach toward me, and beam out his golden, light-filled presence. I called him "the Buddha baby," because he reminded me of photos I

Chapter 9: The Healing Deed

had seen of the golden Buddha.

This is why it was such a surprise to me that, when I returned after having a sabbatical year (during which Henry had entered the preschool), his very capable caregivers were recommending that Henry not continue at the school. Words like "disruptive," "disrespectful," "destructive," and even "impossible" came up in conversations. Because of my history with the family, I asked if I could visit Henry at home and make an independent decision about whether to ask Henry to join our kindergarten.

When I arrived at his home, his mother escorted me to the sandbox where Henry was playing. He had lined up all of his metal construction vehicles in a row. I sat down and smiled. Henry looked me over (no warm smiles now, no golden Buddha baby was visible). One by one, he pointed to the construction machinery, named them, and then drove them around. Soon, his mother invited us into the house for cookies and, before leaving the sandbox, Henry pointed to each one, arched his eyebrows inquiringly and, yes, tested me to see if I could remember the names of his vehicles. This could have been one of my initial cues that Henry was displaying a common trait exhibited often by children who have been exposed to childhood trauma—testing others (sometimes provocatively) to see if they are going to display untrustworthy tendencies.

Henry did attend the mixed-age kindergarten that year and the next, and what ensued was a journey fraught with behaviors that exemplified everything that my colleagues had previously described. The first thing I noticed was how present I had to be at every moment in order to be responsive to all of the nuances of Henry's play. Many times, I felt concern for the well-being of the children and practitioners in the room, and it began to dawn on me that we were being continually tested to see if I/we were going to lose our tempers and react adversely to his behaviors.

I had experienced this kind of unconscious solicitation before from children, while working with a group called "Parents in Crisis." My task with this group was to hold play sessions for children who were in abusive relationships with parents, while the parents were in the next room participating in group counselling sessions. From this experience, I recognized the "testing" gesture that Henry repeatedly portrayed. That gesture was also evident in the group of young children from abusive households who would unconsciously try to solicit behaviors from me that they were experiencing in their own homes. It was here that I learned that my reactions really mattered to these children and that what adults *don't* do in these situations can be a healing deed. Sometimes what we don't do is more important than what we do.

I learned so much more during the years that Henry was my teacher. I studied everything I could get my hands on that sounded even remotely like Henry's way of being. I also steadfastly described Henry's physiognomy to the angels each night. Each day, I would interface with Henry many times and tried many strategies—to redirect, distract, enter into his play, draw him into my work, be creative with picture imaginations, keep him close beside me, and much more.

Soon, a feeling of helplessness began to surround my thinking about him. This was punctuated by frustration and the worry that love for him and his family was simply not enough. Was I holding him back by standing in the way of his family finding another caregiver who could be more effective? With desperation, I redoubled my efforts at describing Henry and seeing him in my mind's eye just before sleep. It was becoming increasingly difficult to practice positivity and objectivity in this exercise. Each night, this picturing of Henry was followed by asking the angels for their help and inspiration.

Then, one day, the kindergarten children were inside at playtime and Henry was shouting loudly while trying to tip another child out of a chair. I remember that I was wearing a full apron as I headed across the room toward the "skirmish." A few steps into my journey, I dropped to my knees when I was overcome by a picture that came into my mind's eye. It was the golden Buddha baby who had greeted me at the kindergarten door in years past! As I knelt there on the floor, Henry came on his hands and knees, crawling across the floor, lay his head on my lap, pulled my apron around him and sobbed. We were there together for many minutes while Henry sobbed and I gently stroked his back. Then he got up and, without any acknowledgement of the moment we had just had together, he went into the children's play with a demeanor that was less frantic and more peaceful than I had yet experienced with him.

This, of course, was not an instant cure. However, from that moment onward, Henry seemed less reactive and, by often giving questioning glances to me, he showed me that he had trust in my assessment of the situation he was questioning. We were growing together! He was practicing mutuality and we came to an understanding. He "let me in" and soon my gentle hand on his shoulder or an arched eyebrow became the gesture that prompted the healing deed.

When Henry had tried successfully with me, then he became more able to model this with the children. However, I still had to be close by for a while to help soften the children's reactiveness and mistrust of him. Fortunately, most children are naturally forgiving.

Henry was a great teacher for me. He taught me about the healing power of modelling perseverance, kindness and goodness. From this experience I learned that a healing way forward is not necessarily something one can cognize with the intellect or even by deepening an understanding of a child's situation. I learned that the way another human being processes trauma does not necessarily "make sense." I learned about the value of accompanying a child with loving kindness while enlisting the help of spiritual beings.

Conclusion

What a privilege it is to be an early childhood educator and to be called upon to fashion our vocation around the lives of those who will be the carriers of the future. My hope is that we do not lose sight of this as we toil our way through the many tasks involved in being in this professional calling. I'm reminded of the words of Kahlil Gibran, "Work is love made visible," and of Rudolf Steiner, "Work is love in action."

The work of an early childhood educator is a glorious way to place our love in the world.

Blessings on all of your past and future healing deeds. They make a difference to our world.

Be the change you want to see in the world.

ENDNOTES

1. Freya Jaffke, "Kindergarten Work and the 'Mantle' of the Child's Life Forces," chapter 4 in *Work and Play in Early Childhood* (Hudson, NY: 1997).

2. Rudolf Steiner, in *A Modern Art of Education*, pointed out that although it is highly necessary that each person should be fully awake in later life, the child must be allowed to remain as long as possible in the peaceful, dreamlike condition of pictorial imagination. He further emphasized that if we allow the child's organism to grow strong in this non-intellectual way, they will rightly develop in later life the intellectuality needed in the world today; see Rudolf Steiner, *A Modern Art of Education: Lectures Presented in Ilkey, Yorkshire, August 5–17, 1923* (Great Barrington, MA: Anthroposophic Press, 2004).

3. Gordon Neufeld PhD, *The Keys to Well-Being in Children and Youth*, keynote address delivered at the European Union Parliament, Brussels, Nov. 13, 2012, https://neufeldinstitute.org/wp-content/uploads/2017/12/Neufeld_Brussels_address.pdf.

4. Gordon Neufeld and Gabor Maté, *Hold On to Your Kids: Why Parents Need to Matter More than Peers*, updated edition (New York: Ballantine Books, 2014).

5. Gabor Maté and Daniel Maté, *The Myth of Normal: Trauma, Illness, and Healing in a Toxic Culture* (New York: Avery, 2022), 127.

6. Peter Levine and Gabor Maté, *In an Unspoken Voice: How the Body Releases Trauma and Restores Goodness* (Berkeley, CA: North Atlantic Books, 2010), 320.

7. Ibid., 319.

8. Peter Levine and Maggie Kline, *Through a Child's Eyes: Awakening the Ordinary Miracle of Healing* (Berkeley, CA: North Atlantic Books, 2006).

9. Rudolf Steiner, *The Education of the Child and Early Lectures on Education* (Hudson, NY: Anthroposophic Press, 1996).

10:
Soul Nutrition
Rihana Rutledge

A four-year-old boy, looking very thoughtful, said, "Mama, when I was going down the rainbow bridge with my angel, did my angel give me rainbow treats to eat?"

When you were coming down the rainbow bridge, did your angel say, "Here are some treats. When you become a teacher, you will need them for nourishment"? The word "nourish" is derived from the Latin word "nutrire," meaning "to feed or cherish."[1] Cherishing yourself, caring for your own well-being, is soul nutrition, the act of being nourished. What are the "rainbow treats" you cherish that enhance your well-being? How do you know when you are out of balance? What nourishes your body, feeds your soul, and nurtures your spirit?

We live in a fast-paced technological world, busily trying to find a work-life balance, and nourishing ourselves is easily overlooked. Life can become stressful, sometimes to the point of fatigue or burnout, which *could* result in illness. Hearing yourself say, "I have given so much; I have no more to give," likely means that your well is running dry. Maybe it is time to slow down and welcome some soul nutrition into your daily life.

When we are responsible for taking care of young children who learn through imitation, it requires that we learn to take care of ourselves.

We need to model a caring attitude. We need to learn how to care for our own forces. What does burnout look like? How do we check in with ourselves?

It is vital, when supporting children's development, to find the courage to know yourself and reflect on the habits that you may want to cultivate that will be good examples for the children to imitate. Like a beautiful garden that needs to be cultivated in preparation for planting, the children need us to care for and prepare the garden of our souls.

The twelve senses play a key role in everyday life and can be used as a helpful checklist for self-awareness, self-reflection, and self-development. To reflect and be self-aware is to "know thyself." According to Rudolf Steiner, "The establishment of twelve senses, each at rest in its own proper region, provided a basis for earthly self-awareness."[2]

The Twelves Senses as a Way of Checking In with Ourselves

Michaela Glöcker, in her book *Education for the Future*, writes, "[W]e have 12 basic sensations at our disposal that give us a healthy feeling of existence, the 'experience of being present,' not only with regards to the environment but also with regards to one's own well-being. In the case of a deficient development, we can make up some things later with the help of perception exercises, bodywork, and artistic therapies."[3]

We can check in with each of our twelve senses and assess which sense is being neglected. Balance is not only physical but also refers to balance in our soul and spiritual realms. You know when you are in balance in any of these three realms. When you are out of balance, it can affect every aspect of your life, like a row of toppling dominos.

Four Senses that Bring the Body into Self-Awareness

The senses of touch, life, self-movement, and balance are also called the *will senses* or the *foundational senses*. These bodily senses will help you recognize the need to pay more attention to your bodily well-being.

Four Senses that Bring the Soul Experience of the Environment into Self-Awareness

The senses of smell, taste, sight, and warmth are also called the *feeling*, *middle*, or *soul senses*. If you feel unbalanced in these senses, it may be an indication that you need to focus on this area.

Four Senses that Serve the Soul-Spiritual Self-Awareness of Coexistence in the World

The senses of hearing, word, thought, and "I" are also called the *social* or *spiritual senses*. If you are aware of a lack of capacity in the social senses, this may be the area where you will want to pay attention.

During sensory experiences, human beings have physical responses and also corresponding soul responses, of which we may be less aware. Dr. Glöckler describes these responses as "soul moods."[4]

Soul Moods for the Twelve Senses

Touch: trust in existence

Life: feeling of harmony

Movement: experience of freedom

Balance: fundamental feeling of inner peace

Smell: feeling of sympathy and antipathy

Taste: aesthetic feeling

Sight: inner light and color sensation

Warmth: moral experience of cold and warmth

Hearing: inwardness, experience of the inner soul space

Word: experience of connections

Thought: experience of connections, structure and order

"I" of the other: experience of "you"

Replenishing Your Physical Forces

Physical well-being means feeling at home in your body. The senses connected to the physical body are the senses of touch, smell, and hearing. Looking at these three senses, which of them calls your attention? Which is not in balance?

The physical body is made up of bones, muscles, and nerves that support movement. Self-expression using whole body movement brings us back into relationship with the body. Going for walks, swimming, and bicycling outdoors can be rejuvenating. Stretching and breathing exercises, yoga, or tai chi can ease tension. Eating nutritious foods and getting regular sleep all contribute to replenishing physical forces. Some therapeutic ways to reconnect with your physical body are singing, music, dance, drama, eurythmy, and rhythmical massages.

When we take care of our physical body, we regain trust and re-establish bodily harmony.

Nourishing Your Etheric Body—Rhythm, Repetition, Reverence

The etheric body promotes growth and regeneration, and follows the laws of life processes, rhythm, and time. You support your life forces when you connect to the senses of life, taste, and word. The etheric body supports the life forces of the physical body, regulating breathing, circulation, and metabolism. Some therapeutic activities to nourish the etheric and rhythmical movement of the heart and lungs are singing, painting, form drawing, clay modeling, cooking, and baking.

Take regular breaks from screens and digital devices to replenish your life forces. Go out into nature—camp, canoe, have picnics, and spend time outdoors. Visiting green spaces, taking walks in the park, experiencing "forest bathing," hiking, gardening, or simply sitting in the garden or by a lake or ocean can be refreshing and soothe overstimulated senses.

The three Rs that we bring to our work with the children can also work healthfully in our own lives. Working with the three Rs reinforces our connection to our environment.

> **Rhythm** within our day brings a sense of calm and inner peace to life.
>
> **Repetition** creates a sense of security by having a consistent structure in your routines.
>
> **Reverence** develops a sense of respect and love for the meaningful tasks you do and the people with whom you are working.

When we take care of our etheric body, we nourish our habit life and gain motivational strength.

Enlivening Your Imagination—Working with the Astral Body

The etheric body follows the laws of rhythm and time, while the astral body follows the laws of differentiation. You support your astral body when you connect to the senses of movement, sight, and thought. The two soul qualities in the astral body are sympathy and antipathy. Sympathy expresses *interest* while antipathy expresses *disinterest*. When these two polarities live in the soul, they affect our thoughts, feelings, and actions. One can be drawn into extremes by being either overreactive or passively frustrated.

In artistic activity we can experience finding balance, harmony, and beauty in the feeling realm. The arts can help us mediate and balance what we experience both in our conscious thought-life and in our unconscious will-life. They help bring to light whatever is living below the level of consciousness on the one hand and, on the other hand, bring strongly formed concepts down into living pictures.

During artistic practice, we are in dialogue with the nature of the medium in which we are working. This requires that we enter into sensing as well as doing. In this way we are also cultivating relational skills, listening as well as speaking and giving as well as receiving. Learning how to mediate our own opposing impulses artistically can potentially help us learn how to find harmony and balance in social situations.

Two other important means of enlivening the imagination are reading lots of fairy tales and poetry. Some teachers keep a book of poetry by their bedside.

When we take care of our astral body, we invite color and beauty into our lives.

Strengthening Your "I"

Balancing life's polarities requires a conscious awakening of the "I." Our "I" can be objective, but this requires open-mindedness, striving to be free of bias or judgement. To be objective, we need to develop authenticity and a healthy sense for the truth. You support your "I"-sense, when you connect to the senses of balance, warmth, and the "I"-sense of the other.

Both children and adults feel valued when they are heard. Suspending judgement allows one's "I" to meet the "I" of the other in reverence and devotion. Listening well and communicating clearly promotes healthy and loving relationships. It is in the inwardness of the soul space one finds equanimity. Balancing sympathy and antipathy in your inner life leads to authenticity and the development of empathy.

When we discover our "I" in the other and the other in us, we access our inner light.

Developing Your Inner Resources

As Betty Staley, in her book *Soul Weaving*, describes the "I"-sense:

> The "I" is the "higher self, the ego, pure spirit." It is the center of soul life. It works like a house in which our "I" lives.

It works through our thinking, our feelings, and our deeds to transform them. The "I" works through thinking so we can connect with spirit, through feeling so we can become conscious of ourselves as individuals, and in actions—the fruits of our will—to express itself in each stage of development. The "I" lives in the house of the human being, forming, shaping, and creating. The manifestation of the "I" in our soul life is our personality.[5]

Some therapeutic considerations for "I" development are meditative practices offered by Rudolf Steiner. The "Review of the Day" is daily meditative practice. Buddha's Eightfold Path is a weekly practice, and Steiner's "Six Basic Exercises" are a monthly practice.[6] Working rhythmically with any of these meditative practices strengthens the "I" and deepens the connection between our inner and the outer world.

Review of the Day

Self-awareness means being conscious of how you show up for your outer life, and self-reflection is your capacity to turn inward. Cultivating a habit of finding a quiet space every day to be in silence, to listen, is essential to soul health. In our nightly review process, we support the deepening of our awareness by reviewing our day (ideally in reverse order) in our imagination for a few minutes before sleeping.

Taking those pictures into our sleep increases our capacity for self-observation. It is important to be as objective as possible and suspend any judgments that may arise as you review your thoughts, feelings, and actions from the day. You may want to do some journal writing if that helps bring your thoughts to consciousness. Notice any words, thoughts, or images that come to you upon waking that are reflections from your review the previous night.

BECOMING AND BELONGING

The Eightfold Path

The Eightfold Path is a weekly practice Rudolf Steiner gave in *Guidance in Esoteric Training*, which offers the opportunity to experience a different qualitative relationship to each day of the week.[7]

- **Monday:** pay attention to one's speaking, to what one says to others, and whether it is authentic and bears meaning.
- **Tuesday:** consider one's actions, that these are not disturbing for others.
- **Wednesday:** live in accordance with nature and spirit.
- **Thursday:** order things, be aware of the boundaries of one's strength, and take care not to go beyond, but also to not leave things undone that lie within them.
- **Friday:** endeavor to learn as much as possible from life, from all one's experiences, from the good and from the bad.
- **Saturday:** pay attention to one's ideas, think only significant thoughts, in order to cultivate memory.
- **Sunday:** become aware of one's decision-making process, determine matters only after thorough deliberation on what speaks for and against them.

Six Basic Exercises

Rudolf Steiner gave the Six Basic Exercises to his students as a means of "clearing the mirrors of our soul." The series of six exercises are practiced daily and typically taken up in succession for a month at a time. After the first month, the second exercise is added, so that in half a year all six exercises have been experienced. A detailed description of the exercises by Rudolf Steiner is in appendix IV of this volume.

(1) Control of thought aims to help you gain control over your thinking process.

(2) Control of will aims to help you gain control over your actions.

(3) Equanimity, or the exercise of feeling, aims to keep you aware of your feelings, to weaken strong ones, strengthen weak ones, and balance them.

(4) Positivity aims to help you see the positive in addition to the bad and the ugly. In this exercise, thinking and feeling are combined.

(5) Open-mindedness aims to keep you always open to new experiences. In this exercise, feeling and willing are combined.

(6) Inner harmony is the sixth, in which the previous exercises need to be practiced to create harmony in thinking, feeling, and willing.[8]

Michael Lipson describes Steiner's Six Basic Exercises in his book, *The Stairway of Surprise,* and advises us not to think of the exercises as work, but as play. "It is up to you to find the best time of day to do them ungrudgingly. Do not think of them as laborious or even as important. You can go into them lightheartedly, with a relaxed body and easy mind. Think of them not as one more added responsibility, but as refreshment."[9] Lipson's book is a wonderful introduction to working with the Six Basic Exercises.

In *Understanding Deeper Developmental Needs,* Dr. Adam Blanning describes the Six Basic Exercises and how they can be useful to Waldorf teachers. "Practicing the whole sequence allows us to model stronger and richer moral capacities in the world and refines our ability to sense the spiritual world (learning to see the good and be open to what is new). It will encourage and reassure the children we work with, as they continuously look to know how to engage with the earthly, physical world."[10]

Biography

"Biography" originated from the medieval Latin word *biographia*, meaning "description of life." In Greek, "bios" means life and "graphia" is a record or account.[11] Biography is an account of significant events and crises a person experienced in their life. It is a creative process to map the significant relationships and the karmic ties to these individuals one has met. Biography work can be helpful for looking at how one's life unfolds in seven-year rhythms. It can support self-awareness and taking responsibility for one's thoughts, feelings, and actions.

Biographical exercises offer a helpful way to reflect on our life journey, deepen our understanding of the phases of human development, and recognize the influences that have shaped our destiny. Each human being undergoes three phases of development from childhood to adulthood—physiological, psychological, and spiritual. The poem below by Mary O'Malley speaks about the virtue of being able to see the wholeness of our lives.

> Life is set up
> to bring up
> what has been bound up
> so it can open up
> to be freed up
> so you can show up for life[12]

Signe Ecklund Schaefer, in her book *Why on Earth* explores the role biographical understanding can play in helping us become more conscious of the purpose and intention of our lives. One her first exercises asks her readers to imagine themselves coming to earth. She asks us to imagine what we packed in our bags in order to become the person we are now. How have each of these things affected our lives?[13]

In her book she delves into each of the seven-year cycles of development (not just the first three cycles from birth to twenty-one) in terms of the various capacities that come forth in each of those periods. For the periods between twenty-one and forty-two, in which the human being is focused primarily on soul development, she describes a set of questions that help us build a vivid picture of the people and events that have had a significant impact on our lives. For example: Did you experience a turning point in those years? How did you make decisions in the different phases? Who were particularly important people for you at this time? What learning did those years offer you?[14]

Biographical questions not only help us understand ourselves better, but they are also great ways to connect with parents and colleagues. In a parent meeting, a teacher could ask parents to recall their favorite kind of play when they were the age of their child. With colleagues, sharing a significant event that brought each of us to choosing teaching as our profession can build warmth and understanding in the faculty circle. Starting with simple questions allows everyone to feel safe. Of course, participation is invited and never compulsory.

Healthy Social Life

Biographical exercises can also help us understand challenging events or relationships. During the last year of Rudolf Steiner's life, he emphasized the importance of working consciously with the idea of karma as a healing force in the world. He suggested that if we examine our life, we can recognize that our challenges have brought us the greatest insights and given us the impetus for growth and development. This recognition can also help us be more compassionate toward others in our lives. The deeper purpose of working consciously with biography and karma is to support individual and societal transformation and healing.

Today it is essential for teachers to recognize the times we live in and our task of fostering healthy social relations in the classroom. This requires cultivating a caring attitude toward engaging with the children on their destiny path and deepening our inner work to support the children as they transition through their developmental phases.

BECOMING AND BELONGING

It is equally essential that teachers pay attention to their adult relationships and our shared social life. "The Motto of the Social Ethic" is a verse given to us by Rudolf Steiner that many faculties and boards regularly bring to their meetings. Learning to work consciously with our colleagues is another way to balance our inner and outer lives.

> *The healing social life is found*
> *When in the mirror of each human soul*
> *The whole community finds its reflection,*
> *And when in the community*
> *The virtue of each one is living.*
>
> —RUDOLF STEINER

This intention and our work together require us to have deep interest in one another, willingness to work on ourselves, and an enduring commitment to our work with the children and families and to the healing of the world we live in. This work is not easy, but when our commitment is clear, our community of colleagues can support each of us in our striving.

Soul nutrition means nourishing your body, feeding your soul, and nurturing your spirit. By finding balance in your physical well-being, you can overcome stagnation. Developing authenticity and a love of truth strengthens your etheric well-being. Showing interest in your development and that of others nurtures your astral well-being. Taking initiative strengthens your "I" so you can be fully present in your life.

The morning and evening thresholds are daily opportunities to acknowledge our spiritual striving. At the end of the day we can give thanks and allow our soul to feel gratitude for everything that has happened. In the morning when we wake, we begin the day with new hope. These simple rituals can ignite the light within that can shine like a beacon for others, especially the children who come to us seeking the warmth of heart that helps them grow into their full humanity.

Chapter 10: Soul Nutrition

ENDNOTES

1 The etymology of "nourish" is from the Latin *nutrire*, to suckle or nourish; Merriam-Webster, "Nourish Definition and Meaning," https://www.merriam-webster.com/dictionary/nourish#word-history.

2 Rudolf Steiner, *The Riddle of Humanity*, Lecture VII, August 12, 1916, Dornach, Switzerland (GA170), https://rsarchive.org/Lectures/GA170/English/RSP1990/19160812p01.html.

3 Michaela Glöckler, *Education for the Future: How to Nurture Health and Human Potential* (Stroud, UK: InterActions, 2020), 75.

4 Ibid., 81.

5 Betty Staley, *Soul Weaving: How to Shape Your Destiny and Inspire Your Dreams* (Gloucestershire, UK: Hawthorn Press, B. 1999), viii–ix.

6 For Steiner's "Six Basic Practices," see appendix IV, "Six Basic Exercises," from *Esoteric Development*, lecture given on December 7, 1905, Berlin.

7 Glöckler, *Education for the Future*, 94.

8 See appendix IV.

9 Michael Lipson, *Stairway of Surprise: Six Steps to a Creative Life* (Great Barrington, MA: Anthroposophic Press, 2002), 18.

10 Adam Blanning, *Understanding Deeper Developmental Needs: Holistic Approaches for Challenging Behaviors in Children* (Great Barrington, MA: Lindisfarne Press, 2017), 122.

11 The etymology of "biography" is from the Greek bi- or bios, meaning life, and -graphia, a "graph" or a written account (Merriam-Webster, "Biography Definition and Meaning," https://www.merriam-webster.com/dictionary/biography#word-history).

12 Mary O'Malley, *What's In The Way Is The Way: A Practical Guide for Waking Up to Life*, (Louisville, CO: Sounds True, 2016).

13 Signe Schaefer, *Why on Earth? The Practice of Becoming Human* (Great Barrington, MA: SteinerBooks, 2013), 5, 138.

14 Ibid.

BECOMING AND BELONGING

11:
The Chalice of Community: The Social Art of the Waldorf Early Childhood Teacher

Holly Koteen-Soulé

The highly desired red wagon was the center of attention in an animated and energetic conversation among the kindergarten children. Thinking that this potential tussle was about who would ride in the wagon, the teacher went to investigate. Who would ride in the wagon was not at all in question. Two children were vying for who would get to pull the wagon. Luckily, a solution was not hard to find. The two would take turns—one pulling and the other child pushing the heavily classmate-laden wagon over the uneven ground of the play yard.

Human beings are social. We need one another. Young human beings, especially, need adults as models and guides. At the same time, humanity is still trying to learn how to live well together. Caring, inclusive communities are rare and inspiring. While natural groupings of family and folk are part of our history, communities that are consciously inclusive are a newer phenomenon and require a different kind of awareness of both self and others. Waldorf communities are examples of conscious communities whose goals encompass both individual self-development and mutual development in our shared social life. In the current context of the widespread stresses of modern life and our reawakening to social justice issues, the challenges of living up to our ideal of a healthy social life are considerable.

Waldorf Early Childhood Teachers as Social Artists

As Waldorf early childhood educators, it is our task to create a place where families, in all of their diverse dimensions, are welcomed, feel at home, and are invited to contribute to the weaving of a rich cultural life. Can we create a community where differences and authenticity are valued over sameness and perfection? Can we be patient with the inevitable messiness of group problem solving and find joy in creating novel solutions together that surprise us all? Are we willing to model genuine interest and empathy for others for our children? Are we willing to set aside space for listening—listening to the children, to ourselves, to others? What do we need to change in ourselves in order to be facilitators of the social arts?

The Special Role of the Community in the First Three Years and Beyond

The young child achieves three significant milestones during the first three years of life. During the first year, children learn to walk because they are growing up in a "Community of Walkers." While the capacity is innate, the child needs to experience walking human beings in the surroundings in order to bring that seed capacity to fruition. This is equally true with regards to a child's learning to speak in the second year of life and then, in the third year, to begin exercising a simple kind of thinking. These archetypal human capacities also require the "Community of Human Speakers" and the "Community of Human Thinkers" as models for their development. Miraculous as these achievements are to parents and teachers, these seeds would not bloom without the impetus that children receive from the human beings in their immediate environment.

This principle is also true, to a slightly lesser degree, in relation to other kinds of learning during the child's first seven years. In the first seven years, the everyday, real-life mirror of community activity supports the development of the child's will, their capacity for "doing," and their ability to take hold of their bodily instrument.

In the second seven years of development, children begin to take hold of their feeling life through a wider circle of relationships and experiences that stretch the child's soul between commonalities and differences, sympathies and antipathies. Through the mirroring of this larger circle, the sense of self and the sense of the other continue to emerge. Again, it is the surrounding community that supports this process.

In the third seven-year cycle, between the ages of fourteen and twenty-one, the simple doing-thinking of the young child and the imaginative feeling-thinking of the grade school child are transformed. Logical, abstract thinking predominates during this period. The influence of adults and how they think has a significant impact on the quality of the young person's developing thinking.

During the first twenty-one years, as the circle of relationships expands from family to school and beyond, the social-emotional development of the individual depends significantly on the qualities living in the adults with whom they are interacting and whether or not those adults are continuing to consciously develop themselves, especially in their social-emotional capacities. After twenty-one, we shift from having been shaped to becoming shapers of our social life.

New Paradigms for Relationships and Community Building

Waldorf education was conceived in the aftermath of World War I. At the heart of the endeavor was a wish to provide a counterbalance to the rising tides of materialism and sectarianism. Rudolf Steiner suggested a non-hierarchical model for the organization of the school in which the teachers would work collaboratively to make decisions and carry the spiritual impulse of the school. This was a very radical imagination, one hundred years ago.

While organizational models have evolved as Waldorf schools proliferated in different parts of the world, this picture of a collaborative circle at the center of the community is an ideal that can still be found in many Waldorf schools. It is still a radical imagination! It values the contribution of each individual's gifts and is based on trust in the group's capacity to work collaboratively in the best interests of the children and the school as a whole.

The imagination of a collaborative circle was given specifically to the teachers as a way of working with their teaching colleagues. However, it can also inspire the quality of any of our relationships in a school community, whether they are coworkers, colleagues, parents, or friends of the school. Respect for and interest in others and a willingness to work together engenders healthy relationships and creative solutions. Community life based on collaboration also has the potential to support social healing for its members and be a model worthy of the children who are growing up within the circle of its influence. This way of working is not without challenges. It requires courage, humility, and the willingness to learn from our mistakes and to practice forgiveness.

When I first became a Waldorf early childhood teacher, it was understood that my role included "educating" the parents as well as the children in my class. In the 1980s, meetings with parents were referred to as Parent Education. While our intention was to help parents understand the underpinnings of Waldorf pedagogy, the label did not support certain aspects of what I would now consider a healthy relationship between parent and teacher.

My colleagues and I began to see the need for reframing our relationship with the parents as partners in our work with the children. This picture places the child in the center of our relationship with the parent and facilitates the understanding that we were caring for the child together. Parents as Partners was our new paradigm and, in my experience, one that warmed and enriched my communications and interactions with parents. We asked questions of each other and shared information that allowed the children to feel held as they moved back and forth between home and school.

In recent years, my colleagues and I have been able to acknowledge that our wish to protect young children from certain kinds of experiences until they were developmentally ready was in some way putting parents and teachers on two different sides of a kind of "wall." The Parents as Partners paradigm also needed to be transformed. We asked ourselves how we could invite parents to help build the protective environment for the children. How could we work more collaboratively? I began inviting parents to be my coresearchers in studying and building the environment, especially the social environment, in our classroom community.

For example, we planned certain aspects of our festivals together, so that the parents felt more integral to the event and not just willing volunteers. We also spoke in our parent evenings about the qualities that we would wish for our grown-up children and how we could nurture the development of those qualities now. I gave parents (in addition to individual conferences) an opportunity to reflect on their experiences of the year and share those reflections with the group as a whole.

This kind of collaboration has become ever more important during our current times, marked as they are by increasing polarization in the realm of social values, a world-wide pandemic, and a reawakening to unresolved issues of diversity, inclusion, and social justice. How can we support building a healthy sense of community with the children in our classrooms, with parents and colleagues in the circle of our own schools, and finally, with individuals and groups in the larger social environments in which our schools are embedded?

These are big questions. However, when there is a clarity of vision and intention, small steps, taken one after another, are significant.

BECOMING AND BELONGING

Our growing awareness as individual educators has an effect, as does the growing awareness of a specific school community on the larger Waldorf movement.

Practical Considerations

What does it mean to be artistic in the social realm? The social life lives between two or more people, a group, or a community. It is what lives in the spaces among us. It is, however, profoundly connected to the qualities of soul that live within each of us—a rich palette of moods, feelings, emotions, and virtues. These qualities within individual members are the substance for the creation of our mutual expectations, communications, and agreements. These mutual creations, like the buildings that house a school, are human-made creations, but unlike the physical school, they are not made of wood or bricks or straw bales. They are built out of soul qualities, primarily, the quality of trust.

When we engage with one another, we are open to the possibility that a "we" can arise from the meeting of our "I" and "you." This is not the same devoted trust and wonder that we witness in the young child encountering the world, but it is related. I can see and learn more about myself through my open-hearted interaction with another human being. My caring, nonjudgmental recognition of other human beings can be supportive to them in their development. In the same way that artists need to have a sense for the materials with which they are working, we need to get to know ourselves and how to meet one another in a more than superficial way in order to create together.

Building Community with the Children in Our Classroom

How are we social artists in our work with the children? We know that warmth and love engender a feeling of security in the children. For most of us this comes naturally. The challenging times and the stresses that many children are currently experiencing indicate that something more is needed. If we think about the community of the classroom as a mirror, the children should be able to see themselves reflected in their surroundings, in the play materials, the stories, and circles. The primary gesture that is needed by the children is *affirmation*. Seeing themselves reflected in the classroom and curriculum is one aspect of this gesture.

Our children also want to know that we see, hear, and care for them. Can we notice when they are upset, feeling left out or distressed, even if they are quiet and do not draw attention to themselves? Can we physically or verbally support them in those situations even when we are uncomfortable and don't know how to handle what just happened? Can we make sure that our rhythm is not so packed that it can't accommodate time for taking care of one another? Is there someone who can help us see what we missed or help us recognize when our own prejudices or unconscious biases are on display?

Affirming each family's culture and traditions could be a new aspect of the typical home visit. Setting the tone for the class working together as a group at the beginning of the year with stories of differences and inclusion will be more positively impactful than a set of rules for the children. The ways in which the teachers communicate and support one another also has a significant effect on the social environment and the children. The practice of affirmation in our work with colleagues is no less important than the practice with the children.

Building Community with Parents and Families

I once heard an experienced early childhood teacher ask a group of teachers in training: "How would what we do change if we trusted the parents?" Her question stayed with me and, over time, became a recognition that trust is really the starting point of our work with parents and not the end point. More recently, a colleague shared with me that she recognized how much parents in our times (as much or even more than their children) need space to "breathe." She makes sure that parents can "breathe out" by leaving spaces in parent meetings for listening to one another and creating opportunities for them to build relationships with one another, as well as with their teacher.

These are examples of what I referred to earlier as changing paradigms in our relationships with parents. Our relationship with parents is not a one-way street. We need to cultivate genuine interest in every family that comprises the circle around the class. This will allow us to maintain a healthy center for the children. It will allow both parent and teacher to be honest, make mistakes, and learn together. This is not easy! In fact, it's downright scary to feel that vulnerable. This is especially true when we want to connect with families who are new to Waldorf or whose background is different from our own, culturally or racially. Courage and humility go well with trust!

It is equally helpful to share with parents what we are doing in everyday terms. Of course, this is easier to do if we have internalized the key principles into our own understanding. However, if we have set an intention for honest communication, then we can gracefully defer when there are questions that we are not able to answer (except with what might be interpreted as a "by the book" explanation) until we have time to do further research. Newer teachers can always ask for help from their more experienced colleagues. Sharing observations, rather than conclusions, is a genuinely effective way to engage with parents in a side-by-side manner. A teacher can learn a great deal from a parent's observations, and the exchange goes a long way to warming the relationship. A grade school colleague shared with me that he used to start his parent conferences by asking the parent how the child is doing at home. Now he starts all his conferences by asking the parent: "How are you doing?"

We must never be tempted to blame the parents. This puts them out of the circle of the community and does damage to what we are trying to build. It will not only hinder our relationship with the parent, but also with the child. For me the key gesture in our work with families is *belonging*. A teacher doesn't confer membership on the families. The teacher and other representatives of the school open the space and invite the families, with their gifts and questions, to join the community. What it means to be a part of this specific community is an ongoing social construction project. In the realm of the soul we are all in a "continuously becoming process."

Conscious Community—A Harbor for Healing

It is clear that there are two seemingly opposing impulses at work in our age. One is the need for each of us to fulfill our individual destiny and the other is to balance individual egoism by creating structures that support our working together toward mutual good. Much of what applies to our relations with parents is also relevant to our collegial relations. However, with our colleagues, we have the additional bond of the common vocation and responsibilities that come with our profession.

Rudolf Steiner spoke to the teachers of the first Waldorf school about the importance of working consciously in trust with one another, despite the obvious and inevitable challenges, and to manifest the spirit of sister/brotherhood that is hovering above us in the spiritual world. This is an ideal that sometimes feels unattainable, given what we witness on a daily basis around us. Steiner was not the only one to ask us to shift our gaze and take whatever steps we can toward a better future for humanity.

In the United States, the ideal of "Beloved Community" has long served as an inspiration for the current generation of social activists. The phrase was first coined by Josiah Royce, the founder of the Fellowship of Reconciliation. Martin Luther King Jr., a member of the Fellowship, spoke often and eloquently about the Beloved Community as a way to meet the challenges of our times. For bell hooks, the African American activist, "Beloved Community is formed not by eradication of difference but by its affirmation, by each of us claiming the identities and cultural legacies that shape who we are and how we live in the world."[1]

A conscious community is a place where we do not have to be perfect, but where we can bring our less-than-whole, imperfect selves with all of our hurts and be received just as we are. Each of us has had this experience in our lives, of being loved and cared for without judgment, whether by human or angelic companions. Healing (and never losing hope for healing) might even be the ultimate purpose of community—healing for each of us and for our body social.

ADDITIONAL RESOURCES

Schaefer, C. *Partnerships of Hope: Building Waldorf School Communities*. Chatham, NY: AWSNA Publications, 2012.

LeadTogether: Resources for Collaboration, Leadership, and School Development. Accessed April 3, 2024. https://www.leadtogether.org.

Koteen-Soulé, H. "The Artistic Meeting: Making Space for Spirit." In *Creating a Culture of Collaborative Spiritual Leadership* by the Pedagogical Section Council of North America. Chatham, NY: Waldorf Publications, 2014. This resource is included as appendix V of this volume.

ENDNOTES

1   bell hooks, *Killing Rage: Ending Racism* (New York: Henry Holt and Company, 1995), 265.

12:
Hope: A Tonic for the Future
Laurie Clark

I had a shocking experience during the Covid quarantine. I was taking a walk. Two little girls who live down the block from me were playing with chalk on the sidewalk. When they saw me coming toward them, they both screamed and ran to their father who was on their front porch. He told them that they had done "a good job." I realized that they must have been told to run away from people out of fear of catching the virus. It pained me to think that these children were being taught to be afraid of people.

The word hopeful means to be full of hope. In Old English, the word hope comes from hopa, which means confidence in the future.

The world, with all of its worries of climate change, war, and political challenges, can be overwhelming. The collective sufferings from prejudices that exist racially, religiously, and in countless other ways in our society cause great pain. The polarization of people over political situations and the many aspects of the pandemic, with the personal distress it has brought, is challenging.

When children are exposed to and confronted with world troubles, it can cause them a great amount of anxiety and distress. The traumatic impact of isolation still casts its shadow on the young child's path of development, along with the fear that Covid carried with it.

BECOMING AND BELONGING

Intellectual explanations about the worries of the world obscure rather than clarify the situation for the young child. The young child thinks in a pictorial way and has no "filters" to shut out the foreboding that lives within these dire situations. The children depend on adults to offer a protective shield around them while still offering them truth within the bounds of hopefulness.

Fred Rogers, the gracious host, for over thirty years, of *Mister Rogers' Neighborhood*, gives us a wonderful example of this kind of hopeful truth that was given to him by his mother in his childhood. When he was a child, his mother showed him ways to find hope in challenging circumstances:

> When I was a boy and I would see scary things in the news, my mother would say to me, "Look for the helpers. You will always find people who are helping." To this day, especially in times of "disaster," I remember my mother's words and I am always comforted by realizing that there are still so many helpers—so many caring people in this world.[1]

This advice from Fred Rogers's mother suffused his whole life with confidence and hope in people. He goes on to say, "I came to see that the world is full of doctors and nurses, police and firemen, volunteers, neighbors and friends who are ready to jump in to help when things go wrong."[2]

Through growing up with this treasure of hope always in his pocket, Fred Rogers was able to reach out to many children and give them the same gift of hopeful truth and confidence in life that his own mother gave to him.

Engendering Hope in the Early Childhood Classroom

What is it that is really needed as we find our way into the future? What are the healing gestures that teachers can provide so that the children in our care can feel safe, secure, and full of trust as they navigate their way through life? How can we engender hope in their lives? The teacher can become a kind of sensing organ to see what is needed to bring assurance to the children.

Hope is something we need to cultivate. It involves the ability to live with uncertainty of the future while still holding the confidence that whatever it brings, we will find a way to meet it. The cultural destiny that we all find ourselves in is calling for us to wake up and meet each unprecedented situation with strengthened inner capacities.

Sometimes it feels impossible to find the way, and yet navigating the unknown is the only choice. We live with uncertainties that are not under our control all the time. How can we learn to live with so many uncertainties? Rabbi Aron Moss suggests a path in a Sabbath blog that he composed:

> It is not that we have lost our sense of certainty. We have lost our illusion of certainty. We never had it to begin with. We never know what the future holds. We have to admit our vulnerability. Close your eyes and feel the uncertainty, make peace with it, let yourself be taken by it. Embrace your cluelessness, and every time you do, remember whose hands you are in.[3]

Hope involves envisioning the future while recognizing that there will be challenges, setbacks, and unknown circumstances to face. The ability to have courage for the future, even when things seem to be moving in the wrong direction, involves the resilience and power of the indomitable human spirit. It enables us to keep going in the face of adversity. When the adult who is with children has assimilated hope into their inmost being, the young child, who learns through imitation, will be able to absorb it because the child has placed their utmost trust in that person. For a child, the starting point for feeling hopeful comes streaming into them from the people they trust.

There are many things that we already do in the classroom which help the children build trust in themselves and others. When we understand how these activities can also soothe and comfort the children, they can be even more nourishing and supportive.

Predictable Rhythm and Routine

Rhythm helps organize the breathing. The healthy sequence of in-breath and out-breath is rhythmic and, when it is in order, it is soothing and settling. When a child feels unsettled, the breath can quicken. When a child cries, deep breaths are taken in, while laughing takes the breath out. In between these two poles lies the sense of stability, in which the deep breath into oneself is balanced with an outbreath into the world. How does one keep a balance of "soul-breathing" in an early childhood classroom? This might look like a group activity alternating with a self-directed creative playtime. How is the pace of activities—too slow, too fast? Are there too many activities or not enough? Are there too many transitions or too few? The teacher holds the delicate balance with loving warmth and carries the task of keeping the equilibrium in the class that promotes a feeling of well-being.

It is essential that the children are carried through the day with a strong and predictable routine. One activity follows the next just as day follows night. Knowing how the day unfolds helps the children learn to self-regulate. There is a certain snack for each day in the early childhood classroom. It is very reassuring to know that every Monday, for example, is rice day. If something appears other than rice, panic may set in, especially for the extremely sensitive child who needs to know what is coming in advance in order to feel secure.

The child who often asks, "What is happening next?" may have anticipatory anxiety. They have excessive worry about future events and can even have panic attacks. Young children cannot verbalize and describe why they have anxiety or where it is coming from. Questioning the young child about where this feeling is coming from can cause even more anxiety. Behaviors of constant apprehension and distress may include a looming sense of worry, extreme cautiousness, feeling distraught, and problems with self-regulation. Often these children need more time than others to prepare for transitions between activities. The teacher can let the child know, before the rest of the class, what will happen next. Preparing these children before transitions gives them an opportunity to "catch their breath," and providing them the gift of extra time can help them avoid being overwhelmed. The old saying, "All things come to those who wait," is something to keep close. This kind of empathy by the caregiver for the child's soul situation is a welcome gesture that provides the child relief.

Creative Movement Possibilities

In the first seven years of life, the child's task is to become comfortable in their body. For children who have sensory sensitivities, we try to imagine how this feels. It might be similar to moving into a new house with everything in boxes that are unmarked—we cannot find what we are looking for. This can cause frustration, which in turn, can cause other unusual behaviors.

If a child has experienced trauma, the child may only be able to cope by disassociation, by losing contact with themselves and the world. The child can have a kind of soul soreness and feel excluded. They may "move away" from themselves through aggression or depression. These children may feel stuck and unable to move from one soul state to another. There can be a sense of disorientation that makes it difficult to make sense of how life works.

We can find ways to be creative with these children who have had trauma and are experiencing painful soul movement. The teacher needs to carry extreme sensitivity and understanding with these children. It is important to help them find interest in daily life. Inviting the child to help with cooking and baking, washing the dishes in warm water together with the teacher, or sweeping the room together gives the child the ability to move. When we accompany the child in this way, it lifts their heaviness of soul, gives them mobility, and assures them of the goodness of life, that all is well.

BECOMING AND BELONGING

Humor also is a lifting gesture for all children. It is important to bring developmentally appropriate silly things that make the children laugh. Laughter is a breathing out, a kind of letting go. An example: a child tells me their nose is running; "Oh," I might say, "I better chase it before it gets away!" In a circle, humor might come in the little chickadee verse. "On a hazel branch I spied three little chickadees side by side. On the left is Felix, on the right is Hans, and smack in the middle is *Smartypants!*" A little bit of naughtiness can be hilarious to the young child.

Circle time in the early childhood class provides many benefits. We all face one another in a circle, and everyone is welcomed and warmly greeted. It takes cooperation to move together. We all need to move in the same direction, hold hands, and become somewhat aware of our friends. Circle time is a community-building activity; we move, sing, and recite all together. This activity requires cooperation with others and plants the first seeds of a healthy social life. The very first experiences of being helpers to our friends begins in the circle.

Spatial awareness, motor planning, balance, and body geography can all be integrated into the circle adventure to give the children lots of movement opportunities. This is all surrounded with seasonal imaginations that weave a story motif which enhances the movement.

Free Drawing

When a child is allowed to draw freely with no instruction from an adult, they are able to express many things. This activity gives the child the opportunity to express their relationship to the world. Through their drawings, children can depict things that they are not able to verbalize, including their thoughts, feelings, and worries. If the child has had a traumatic event in their life, drawing can become a therapeutic tool to "draw" out what would otherwise remain unspoken. Giving children a safe space to express themselves can be freeing and allow the children to bring out on paper what they are inwardly experiencing. Sometimes the pictures that the children draw are full of joy, and at other times they display soul stress.

The pictures that a child draws gives us indications of the child's situation, developmentally, emotionally, culturally, and even physically. Free drawing is a creative process and a safe means for powerful feelings to come to the surface. The teacher notices but does not comment on what the child draws. We are offering the child a chance to express themselves with unconditional acceptance.

We can look at the child's drawings without preconceived ideas and from many perspectives. To develop an integral view of what the drawings might represent is a study in itself. Observation and contemplation of these drawings with an openness may bring the teacher deeper understanding of what the child is trying to express.

Watercolor Painting

The movement of the paintbrush across the paper creating flowing color is an elixir for the soul of the young child. When the atmosphere of the classroom reflects a quiet mood, this enhances the inner experience. The flow of color on the wet page moves through the very being of the child and calms them. Painting anchors the sense of well-being.

Little children are so open that they experience the inner quality of color. They feel each color's intrinsic nature. Even the youngest children thrive when they have the opportunity to experience a paint brush dipped into the world of colors. Watercolor painting immerses the child in feeling, they "drink" in the color. It is a nourishing activity that soothes the child's soul.

Festival Life

Festival life plays an integral role in early childhood and throughout life. These celebrations remind us of the wonder of how the human being, nature, and the spiritual world all work together. We are all citizens of the earth and of the spirit.

In the fall the days become shorter, the dark nights become longer, and nature dies away. The trees are bare, the flowers have gone back to Mother Earth, and the gardens are asleep. The sun's power seems to lessen, but our inner light seems to grow brighter. We make a house for our lantern light that will shine like the stars do in the heavens. In community with our family and friends, we bravely go out into the dark night, carrying our precious light in its house and singing together as we walk along. Together, in community, we will find our way.

Our hope is that we will carry this inner lantern light for the rest of our lives. In the future, when uncertainty presents itself in challenging situations, we can find spirit courage and give spirit courage to others. This is how wonder in the festivals ignites our life and illuminates living images that can guide us.

Other festivals during the course of the year partner our everyday life with cosmic rhythms. They are touchstones to our essence as individuals and give meaning to our shared lives when we celebrate together in community.

Fairy Tales

Sharing fairy tales with young children is like giving them a very beautifully wrapped gift. As the teacher tells the story, the child unwraps this present, one image after another. In their imaginations, the children "try on" each of the characters and situations as they hear the story.

Often these stories present three very difficult, seemingly impossible tasks that must be done in order for the protagonist to arrive at the intended goal. It is significant that in many of these stories there are helpers that come to the aid of the one who has taken on the adventure. More often than not, the protagonist has done a good deed for the helper who later returns the favor. This kind of theme runs through fairy tales in a variety of cultures.

An example of this is in the Grimm's fairy tale "The White Snake." One day a boy comes across three fishes caught in the reeds and gasping for water. Being kind, he frees them. The fishes say to him, "We will remember you and repay you for saving us!" Later, the king throws a golden ring into the sea and says that the boy must find it or he will be thrown back into the sea until he can fetch it out. The three fishes come to his rescue and dive deep into the sea. They bring up a mussel, and when the boy opens it, he finds the golden ring that he needed. It is interesting that the mussel needs to be opened in order to secure the golden ring. Gold is a kind of compressed sun material, and it also represents wisdom and can be used as a remedy for heart conditions. Symbolically, opening the mussel can be a picture of opening our heart, which is just what is needed in order to find the treasure (golden ring) which lies within it. How often do we find ourselves in such a situation, where in order to find our way through a difficulty, we must dive down into the inmost part of our soul? Then, with the help of our spiritual helpers, we open our heart in such a way that the "treasure" is found.

The resilience and fortitude of the one who has these unbelievably hard tasks that need to be performed is a wonder! The characters in the fairy tales overcome their difficulties and become transformed in the process. How in the world can that happen? It seems beyond human capacity to endure and find the way through such challenges. How often in our own lives have we experienced that the tasks we have to face are beyond what we think we can possibly do? And yet, with spirit courage we go forward, not knowing how things will turn out. It is a marvel how perseverance through adversity, with the intention of doing good in the world, makes one stronger. The children hear the story, picture themselves, and deeply feel that they are able to achieve these victories. The perseverance, resilience, and courage contained in these tales are all needed as ingredients to fortify hope for the future.

Fairy tales strengthen the heart and the forces of the soul. These stories bring an inner security and reassurance to the child despite

BECOMING AND BELONGING

the harmonies and disharmonies of life. Fairy tales give children encouragement for the present and remain a living force throughout their lives.

Strengthening Our Inner Capacities with Spiritual Hope

What is awakened in the human being in a time of difficulty is the predisposition to make contact with the spiritual world, the invisible guidance within one's destiny.

—ORLAND BISHOP

The teacher creates the atmosphere for the children in their care. Just as the sun warms and lights our world, the teacher can bring a warming light into the classroom. If there are unacceptable, difficult conditions that the teacher needs to guide the children through, because there is no other choice, what is the most important thing the teacher can do? What is necessary to reassure the children in our care?

A true account of a man named Janusz Korczak gives us a remarkable illustration of the creation of spiritual hope in the direst of circumstances. On November 30, 1940, in Poland, two hundred children, with adults accompanying them, were walking in a celebratory procession. It was a wondrous sight. All the children were beautifully dressed in colorful clothes and walked two by two in an orderly fashion. They carried pictures they had painted and cages of singing birds. The children were also singing, playing musical instruments, and reciting poetry. They were led by a small man with gray hair named Janusz Korczak.

This was the day that all Jews were ordered into the ghetto. Janusz was a pediatrician and educator who lived his whole life in service to children. He worked for decades to create the orphanage that was a home to the children walking in this procession. The orphanage was beautifully designed to serve the children in his care, and they lived happily there. He wrote petitions to exempt the children from the ghetto, but all in vain.

Chapter 12: Hope: A Tonic for the Future

He felt that this moment when the orphans left the home they had known and loved should be beautiful and associated with joy. Janusz looked for the sources of joy that were available in that moment so that strength could flow into the children. He was able, for the children's sake, to achieve a mood of hope. He did not allow the circumstances that they faced to pull them down.

This procession is famous and still remembered in Poland. Even though the ghetto offered inadequate housing and insufficient sources of food, Janusz tried to beautify the children's ghetto house with flower boxes and by putting the children's drawings on the walls. He created a school for the children. They did plays, art, singing, and reciting, activities similar to a Waldorf curriculum. He suffered greatly under the Nazi regime but tried to find hope in small things to keep his morale up for the sake of the children. The depth of his love coupled with his revolutionary spirit kept the children sheltered under his care for as long as was possible.

In a lecture entitled "Faith, Love and Hope," Rudolf Steiner implores us to embrace and permeate ourselves with spiritual hope.[4] Steiner goes on to say, "The forces of hope are life-giving and bring confidence for the future. We cannot take a single step in life without the force of hope. We actually know nothing about the following day, even whether or not we will be alive. We know about the future just as much as we need to know. Life would be impossible in the physical world were not future events to be preceded by hope. Would anyone sow seeds if we had no idea what would become of them?"

Hope counteracts uncertainties; it provides a powerful antidote to despondency. It enlivens us to take steps toward the future knowing that our plans might need to completely change before we get to where we thought we were going. Flexibility and adaptability at every turn is what is needed now. To bathe one's soul with spiritual hope provides an inner gesture of healing and will be a gift to the children in our care. Permeation with hopefulness enkindles warmth and vitality within us. This precious inner soul warmth brings comfort to others, even in the most difficult of situations. It gives us the potential to courageously face the circumstances that the unknown future might hold at any given time.

The spiritual hope that we hold in our hearts can be infused through the advice given by Henning Köhler in his book *Difficult Children—There Is No Such Thing*.[5] He prescribes certain qualities that the teacher needs to develop in order to help the children in their care who have experienced trauma. Protecting attentiveness, comforting trust, and accompanying interest are the qualities that work together to provide the understanding that many children so desperately need.

Protecting attentiveness requires the teacher to be creative in their understanding and to "listen in," with deep devotion and reverence, to what each child needs. The teacher adapts a quiet and alert attention without a lot of talking about it with the children. This kind of inner listening gives a picture of what is needed, initiating a sense of "listening acknowledgment" that embraces the children.

Accompanying interest involves being there for the child and patiently standing at the child's side with a waiting attitude. Trauma and anxiety do not disappear quickly, but accompanying the child creates the quality of being deeply interested and involved. It will give the child the gift of time without expecting that they will hurry through their ordeal or change in any way. This kind of participation from the teacher is subtle but powerful and follows the process of the child's development without demanding results.

Comforting trust is perhaps the most important of all. The emotions that the child carries need to be met by the teacher with empathy and confirmation. One of the most important ways to establish comfort and trust is providing all of the healthy things we know to do for the young child. A strong and predictable rhythm, nourishing food, homelike activities, and time in nature create security and well-being. In these times, simplifying and reducing our transitions could be helpful, especially for the sensitive children in our care. However, the most comforting way to establish trust is to ask for help from the child's angel. This is the key that opens the door to true comfort and will instill the deepest trust between the child and teacher.

Henning Köhler describes healing as "[not] an elimination of illness but rather guidance to the essential. Healing means giving hope, to give hope means to have hope. A person's hopeful thinking about a person is loving thinking."[6]

Nature: Hopeful Images

Sometimes nature gives us an image of the profound mystery of hope. In Olympic National Park in Washington State, there is a Sitka spruce tree, the largest kind of spruce, growing on the beach. It is unique because it grows on the edge of a sandy bluff between two cliffs. Erosion has taken all of the soil away, and the roots seem to supply the tree with life even though it has no soil. The roots hang in midair, not secured in the earth, and yet the tree continues to have evergreen foliage on the top. Even with its roots exposed, it goes on living against all odds.

It has been called the Tree of Life because it is like no other. So far, it has remained alive against all odds. Intense storms with wind and rain have not toppled it yet. It holds on the best that it can with what it has to work with, asking for nothing more. Many people wonder if it has some kind of magical quality.

Perhaps it is called the Tree of Life because it is symbolic of what we sometimes live through. When we experience traumatic, unbearable circumstances in our lives, it may feel like we are hanging on by just a few threads, in midair with no ground beneath us. Like the Sitka spruce, we hang on.

Spiritual hope brings the warmth force that is needed in these times. Carrying hope in our arms as an offering to the children will gracefully pave the way into the future. An exquisite image in Greek mythology is the goddess Elpis, who is the spirit of hope. She is depicted as a young woman, usually carrying flowers or a lighted

BECOMING AND BELONGING

lamp in her hands. The flowers in her arms have blossomed from the seeds of her heart, and the small light that she carries leads the way through the unknown.

*Vintage woodcut depiction of Hope
(courtesy of Christine Kohler via iStock)*

Chapter 12: Hope: A Tonic for the Future

Either we have hope within us or we do not.

It is a dimension of the soul and is not essentially dependent on some particular observation of the world.

Hope is an orientation of the spirit, an orientation of the heart. It transcends the world that is immediately experienced and is anchored somewhere beyond its horizons.

Hope in this deep and powerful sense is not the same as joy that things are going well or willingness to invest in enterprises that are obviously headed for early success, but rather an ability to work for something because it is good, not because it stands a chance to succeed.

Hope is definitely not the same thing as optimism. It is not the conviction that something will turn out well, but certainty that something makes sense regardless of how it turns out.

It is Hope, above all, which gives the strength to live and continually try new things.

—VACLAV HAVEL

The epigraph to the section "Strengthening Our Inner Capacities with Hope" is from "Whitsun: Five Good Words," published on the website of the Anthroposophical Society in America. The final epigraph is found in many online publications. Vaclav Havel was a Czech statesman, writer, and political dissident who became the first president of the Czech Republic in 2003.

ENDNOTES

1. Mr. Rogers first wrote this comforting piece of advice in 1986, according to the *Dominion Post* in West Virginia: "In the Words of Mr. Rogers, 'Look for the Helpers,'" March 18, 2020, https://www.dominionpost.com/2020/03/18/in-the-words-of-mr-rogers-look-for-the-helpers/.

2. Ibid.

3. Aaron Moss, "I've Lost My Sense of Certainty …", Chabad.org, March 13, 2020, https://www.chabad.org/library/article_cdo/aid/4677840/jewish/Ive-Lost-My-Sense-of-Certainty.htm.

4. Rudolf Steiner, "Faith, Love, and Hope," two lectures given at Nurnberg, Germany, December 2–3, 1911, GA130.

5. Henning Köhler, *Difficult Children—There Is No Such Thing: An Appeal for the Transformation of Educational Thinking* (Fair Oaks, CA: Association of Waldorf Schools of North America, 2003).

6. Ibid., 134.

APPENDICES

I. The Essentials of Waldorf Early Childhood Education

Susan Howard

The following article was written for Waldorf early childhood educators and mentors. It has been published frequently, most notably in Mentoring in Waldorf Early Childhood Education (Waldorf Early Childhood Association of North America, 2007). It has been revised and updated for this appendix.

Is there a Waldorf early childhood "curriculum?" Are there specific activities—perhaps puppet plays or watercolor painting, for example—that are required in a Waldorf program? Are there certain materials and furnishings—lazured, soft-colored walls, handmade playthings, natural materials, beeswax crayons—that are essential ingredients of a Waldorf setting? What is it that makes Waldorf early childhood education "Waldorf?" Rudolf Steiner spoke on a number of occasions about the essentials of education and of early childhood education. His words shed light on what he considered fundamental:

> Essentially, there is no education other than self-education, whatever the level may be. This is recognized in its full depth within Anthroposophy, which has conscious knowledge through spiritual investigation of repeated Earth lives. Every education is self-education, and as teachers we can

> only provide the environment for children's self-education. We have to provide the most favorable conditions where, through our agency, children can educate themselves according to their own destinies. This is the attitude that teachers should have toward children, and such an attitude can be developed only through an ever-growing awareness of this fact.[1]

Thus the essential element in early childhood education is actually the educator, who shapes and influences the children's environment, not only through the furnishings, activities, and rhythms of the day, but most important, through the qualities of their own being and relationships: with the children and other adults in the kindergarten or early childhood setting, with the parents, to daily life in the kindergarten, and to living on earth.

These qualities, which include attitudes and gestures both outer and inner, permeate the early childhood setting and deeply influence the children, who take them up through a process of imitation. The results of such experiences appear much later in the child's life through predispositions, tendencies, and attitudes toward life's opportunities and challenges.

Viewed in this way, early childhood education demands an ongoing process of self-education by the adult. If we again ask, what makes a Waldorf program "Waldorf," the answers might be sought less in the particular activities or rhythms or materials and furnishings, and more in the extent to which these outer aspects are harmonious expressions of inner qualities, attitudes, capacities, and intentions of the teacher—all of which can have a health-giving effect on the children, both in the moment and for the rest of their lives.

Those of us who are committed to this path of Waldorf early childhood education, whether as early childhood teachers or mentors, may actively ask ourselves how qualities essential to the healthy development of young children are living in our own early childhood groups, in our own daily lives, and in our own inner practice.

Rudolf Steiner spoke on a number of occasions about experiences essential for healthy early childhood education, including the following:

- Love and warmth
- Care for the environment and nourishment for the senses
- Creative, artistic experience
- Meaningful adult activity as an example for the child's imitation
- Free, imaginative play
- Protection for the forces of childhood
- Gratitude, reverence, and wonder
- Joy, humor, and happiness
- Adult caregivers on a path of inner development

The following brief descriptions of these qualities and related questions are intended to serve the self-reflection of the individual teacher, the observations of the mentor, and the process of helpful, open dialogue between mentor and mentee.

Love and Warmth

Children who live in ... an atmosphere of love and warmth, and who have around them truly good examples to imitate, are living in their proper element.[2]

Love and warmth, more than any programmatic approach to early education, create the basis for development. These qualities are expressed in the gestures that live between adult and child, in the children's behavior toward one another, and also in the social relations among the adults in the early childhood center. In other words, they form the social community of early childhood education and can foster a sense of belonging. When Rudolf Steiner visited the classes of the first Waldorf school, he was known to ask the school children, "Do you love your teacher?"

Questions we can ask ourselves and discuss in mentoring conversations include the following:

- Are love and warmth living in the atmosphere?
- How are they expressed in the gestures that live between adult and child?
- How are they expressed in the children's behavior toward one another?
- How are the social relations among the adults caring for the children?
- What hindrances exist to creating a loving atmosphere?
- How is love expressed in the teacher's response to "inappropriate" behavior (excessive noise, aggression, disruptions, conflict)?

Less apparent within the day, but also of great significance, are these same qualities of love and warmth in relations with colleagues outside the classroom, with the parents, and with the wider community:

- How are the relations between the early childhood educators and the parents?
- How are the relations with the other colleagues in the early childhood groups and in the rest of the school?
- How does the teacher work with conflict and difficulties with adults?
- Are the children surrounded by a community that offers love and warmth and support?

Care for the Environment and Nourishment for the Senses

> The essential task of the kindergarten teacher is to create the proper physical environment around the children ... "Physical environment" must be understood in the widest sense imaginable. It includes not just what happens around children in the material sense, but everything that occurs in their environment—everything that can be perceived by their senses, that can work on the inner powers of children from the surrounding physical space. This includes all moral or immoral actions, all the meaningful and meaningless behaviors that children witness.[3]

Early learning is profoundly connected to the child's own physical body and sensory experience. Thus the physical surroundings, indoors and outdoors, should provide nourishing, diverse opportunities for the child's active self-education. By integrating diverse elements and bringing them into a meaningful, understandable and harmonious order, the adult provides surroundings that are accessible to the young child's understanding, feeling, and active will. Such surroundings provide the basis for the development of a sense of coherence. The child unconsciously experiences the love, care, intentions, and consciousness expressed through the *outer* furnishings and materials of the classroom. The *inner* qualities offer a moral grounding for the child's development; the environment is "ensouled" and nurturing.

The adult shapes not only the spatial environment, but also the temporal environment, creating a loving, lively yet orderly "breathing" through rhythm and repetition. Through this healthy breathing process, the child gains a sense of security and confidence in his or her relationship with the world.

Here we can ask:

- Does the environment of the early childhood program offer these qualities of order, care, transparency, and meaning? What is expressed through the outer furnishings and materials?

- Does the space offer diverse opportunities for nourishing experiences in the realm of touch, self-movement, balance, and well-being?

- Are the activities of the day integrated in time into a healthy flow, in which transitions are as smooth and seamless as possible?

- Are there opportunities for lively, joyful physical movement as well as for more inward, listening experience? for large-group, small-group, and solitary experiences?

Creative, Artistic Experience

[I]n order to become true educators, the essential thing is to be able to see the truly aesthetic element in the work, to bring an artistic quality into our tasks.... If we bring this aesthetic element, we then begin to come closer to what the child wills out of its own nature.[4]

In the early childhood class, the art of education is the art of living. Teachers are artists in how they perceive and relate to the children and the activities of daily life. The educator "orchestrates" and "choreographs" the rhythms of each day, the week, and the seasons in such a way that the children can breathe freely within a living structure. In addition, the educator offers the children opportunities for artistic experiences through song and instrumental music, movement and gesture (including rhythmic games and eurythmy), speech and language (including verses, poetry, and stories), modeling, watercolor painting and drawing, puppetry and marionettes.

Here we may ask:

- How do the arts live in the kindergarten, in the teacher, and in the children?

- How is the rhythmic flow of time formed?

- Is the teacher engaged artistically in the domestic arts and work processes?

- How is creative, artistic experience of the child fostered through the furnishings and play materials of the kindergarten?

- Is the play of the children creative and artistic in its imagery, its social interactions, its processes?

- Is the teacher's work with individual children both practical and imaginative? What kinds of imaginations inform their work?

- Is the teacher engaged in creative artistic endeavors? Are they striving to deepen their own understanding and experience of what it means to be artistic?

Meaningful Adult Activity as an Example for the Child's Imitation

> The task of the kindergarten teacher is to adapt the practical activities of daily life so that they are suitable for the child's imitation through play.... The activities of children in kindergarten must be derived directly from life itself rather than being "thought out" by the intellectualized culture of adults. In the kindergarten, the most important thing is to give children the opportunity to directly imitate life itself.[5]
>
> Children do not learn through instruction or admonition, but through imitation.... Good sight will develop if the environment has the proper conditions of light and color, while in the brain and blood circulation, the physical foundations will be laid for a healthy sense of morality if children witness moral actions in their surroundings.[6]

Real, meaningful, purposeful work, adjusted to the needs of the child, is in accordance with the child's natural and inborn need for activity and is an enormously significant educational activity. Thus, rather than offering contrived projects and activities for the children, educators focus on their own meaningful work through activities that nurture daily and seasonal life in the classroom "home": cooking and baking, gardening, laundry and cleaning, creating and caring for the materials in the surroundings, and the bodily care of the children.

This creates a realm, an atmosphere, of freedom in which the individuality of each child can be active. It is not intended that the children copy the outer movements and actions of the adult, but rather that they experience the inner work attitude: the devotion, care, sense of purpose, intensity of focus, and creative spirit of the adult. And then, in turn, each child is free to act as an artist-doer in their own right, through creative free play and active movement, according to their own inner needs and possibilities.

As we observe an early childhood class, we may ask ourselves:

- How does meaningful adult activity live in the group, both indoors and out?
- Do the educators seem able to devote themselves inwardly and outwardly with enthusiasm, in an artistic way, to real life activities and adult work?
- Does the educator appear engaged artistically in a creative process?
- Are the educators' activities truly meaningful and purposeful, in a logical sequence that the child can grasp?
- Do the children imitate the adult's work through their play (not necessarily the outer actions, but perhaps more importantly through the inner gesture of the adult's work)?
- What qualities are expressed in the children's play?

Free, Imaginative Play

> In the child's play activity, we can only provide the conditions for education. What is gained through play stems fundamentally from the self-activity of the child, through everything that cannot be determined by fixed rules. The real educational value of play lies in the fact that we ignore our rules and regulations, our educational theories, and allow the child free rein.[7]

And then, a seemingly contradictory indication:

> Giving direction and guidance to play is one of the essential tasks of sensible education, which is to say of an art of education that is right for humanity.... Early childhood educators must school their own observation in order to develop an artistic eye, to detect the individual quality of each child's play.[8]

Little children learn through play. They approach play in an entirely individual way, out of their own unique configuration of soul and spirit, and out of their own unique experiences in the world they live in. In addition, the manner in which each child plays may offer a picture of how they will take up their destiny as an adult.

The task of the early childhood educator is to create an environment that supports the possibility for healthy play. This environment includes the physical surroundings, furnishings, and play materials; the social environment of activities and social interactions; and the inner/spiritual environment of thoughts, intentions, and imaginations held by the adults.

We may ask the following questions relating to the children's play in the kindergarten or early childhood setting:

- What is the quality and duration of the children's play? Is it active, dynamic, healthy, creative? Are the children self-directed and deeply engaged, socially and individually?

- How does the early childhood educator reconcile these two seemingly contradictory challenges: to give free rein to the child at play, and to guide and direct and provide the conditions for healthy play to develop?

- What are the themes and images of free play?

- Do the play materials offer diverse and open-ended possibilities for creativity, social interaction, and bodily movement?

- Are there opportunities for a wide range of play activities outdoors? How are the children active outdoors, compared with indoors? How much time is there for indoor vs. outdoor play?

Protection for the Forces of Childhood

> Although it is highly necessary that each person should be fully awake in later life, the child must be allowed to remain as long as possible in the peaceful, dreamlike condition of pictorial imagination in which his early years of life are passed. For if we allow the child's organism to grow strong in this non-intellectual way, they will rightly develop in later life the intellectuality needed in the world today.[9]

The lively, waking dream of the little child's consciousness must be allowed to thrive in the early childhood group. This means that the educator refrains as much as possible from verbal instruction; instead, their gestures and actions provide a model for the child's imitation, and familiar rhythms and activities provide a context where the need for verbal instruction is reduced. Simple, archetypal imagery in stories, songs, and games provides "digestible" experiences that do not require intellectual or critical reflection or explanation.

Here we may ask ourselves as educators:

- Does the atmosphere in the room foster an imaginative, not-yet-intellectually-awakened consciousness in the children?

- Are the children allowed to immerse themselves fully in play without unnecessary instruction and verbal direction from the adults?
- Are play processes allowed to run their course, or are they interrupted?
- Does a "group consciousness" prevail in group activities, or are children singled out for special privileges and "turns" and offered choices?
- Do the sequence and rhythms of the day carry the children along, or do the children ask what is coming next?
- Does the educator invite children to participate in activities such as rhythmic circles or finger games through their own activity, or do they wait to see if children are "ready" or verbally explain what is coming?

An Atmosphere of Gratitude, Reverence, and Wonder

> An atmosphere of gratitude should grow naturally in children through merely witnessing the gratitude the adults feel as they receive what is freely given by others, and in how they express this gratitude ... If a child says "thank you" very naturally—not in response to the urging of others, but simply through imitating—something has been done that will greatly benefit the child's whole life. Out of this an all-embracing gratitude will develop toward the whole world. This cultivation of gratitude is of paramount importance.[10]

Out of these early all-pervading experiences of gratitude, the first tender capacity for love, which is deeply embedded in each and every child, begins to sprout in earthly life.

> If, during the first period of life, we create an atmosphere of gratitude around the children ... then out of this gratitude

> toward the world, toward the entire universe, and also out of thankfulness for being able to be in this world ... a profound and warm sense of devotion will arise ... upright, honest and true.[11]

This is the basis for what will become a capacity for deep, intimate love and commitment in later life, for dedication and loyalty, for true admiration of others, for fervent spiritual or religious devotion, and for placing oneself wholeheartedly in the service of the world.

And so we may ask:

- How do gratitude, reverence, and wonder live in the kindergarten?
- Do they come to natural expression from adults and children?
- Are they spontaneous and sincere, or sentimentalized?
- Or if these qualities seem to be missing, how does their absence manifest?

Joy, Humor, and Happiness

> The joy of children in and with their environment must therefore be counted among the forces that build and shape the physical organs. They need teachers who look and act with happiness and, most of all, with honest, unaffected love. Such a love that streams, as it were, with warmth through the physical environment of the children may be said to literally "hatch out" the forms of the physical organs.[12]

> If you make a surly face so that a child gets the impression you are a grumpy person, this harms the child for the rest of its life. What kind of school plan you make is neither here nor there; what matters is what sort of person you are.[13]

Here we may explore the following questions as educators:

- Do happiness and joy live in this group of children and adults?
- What are the most joy-filled aspects of the work?
- Which aspects of the work are least permeated with joy?
- How is the educator's earnestness and serious striving held in a dynamic balance with humor, happiness, and "honest, unaffected love?"
- Are there moments of laughter and delight in the room? How does humor live in the community of children and adults?

Adult Caregivers on a Path of Inner Development

> For the small child before the change of teeth, the most important thing in education is the teacher's own being.[14]

> Just think what feelings arise in the soul of the early childhood educator who realizes: what I accomplish with this child, I accomplish for the grown-up person in his twenties. What matters is not so much a knowledge of abstract educational principles or pedagogical rules.... What does matter is that a deep sense of responsibility develops in our hearts and minds and affects our world view and the way we stand in life.[15]

Here we come to the spiritual environment of the early childhood setting: the thoughts, attitudes, and imaginations living in the adult who cares for the children. This invisible realm that lies behind the outer actions of the educator has a profound influence on the child's development.

The spiritual environment includes recognition of the child as a threefold being—of body, soul and spirit—on a path of evolutionary development through repeated earth lives. This recognition provides a foundation for the daily activities in the kindergarten and for the relationship between adult and child.

BECOMING AND BELONGING

In addition to the questions we have already pondered above, we may ask:

- How is the adult actively engaged in inner development, as an early childhood educator and as a human being?
- How is the educator cultivating a relationship to the children on a spiritual basis?
- How is the educator working with colleagues to foster an environment of spiritual striving and a deepened study of child and human development?
- Does the educator strive to approach their work in such a way that the children in their care are not burdened by unresolved issues in the educator's personal life?
- Do goodness and moral uprightness stream from the being of the teacher? Is their inner and outer activity in coherence with healthy social and ethical values? Is the educator striving to be an example worthy of the children's imitation?
- Does the educator love the children? Do they work to create healthy, caring relationships with the parents, with colleagues, and with the community? Do they love the earth, and the world into which the children are incarnating?
- How does the educator see their own relationship to the past, the present, and the future of our human journey?

This is the very challenging realm of self-knowledge and the activity of the individual ego of the adult—a realm where it is difficult to be objective in our observations. Yet ultimately it is this realm that may affect the development of the children most profoundly. It is not merely our outer activity that affects the developing child; it is what lies behind and is expressed through this outer activity. Ultimately the most profound influence on the child is who we are as human beings—and who and how we are becoming.

Conclusion

The so-called "essentials" described here are qualitative in nature. For the most part, they do not characterize a body of "best practices"; instead, they describe inner qualities and attributes of the adult that foster healthy development in young children. These qualities can come to expression in a wide variety of ways, according to the age range and particular characteristics of the children in a particular group; the nature of the particular program (a kindergarten or playgroup or extended care program, for example); or the environment and surroundings (urban or rural, home or school or child care center, for example).

Many practices that have come to be associated with Waldorf early childhood education—certain rhythms and rituals, play materials, songs, stories, even the colors of the walls or the dress of the adults or the menu for snack—may be mistakenly taken as essentials. The results of such assumptions can be a "King Winter" nature table appearing in a tropical climate in "wintertime," or having only dolls with pink skin and yellow hair. Such practices may express a tendency toward a doctrinal or dogmatic approach that is out of touch with the realities of the immediate situation and instead imposes something from "outside."

There is a parallel concern at the other end of the spectrum from the doctrinal or dogmatic. The freedom that Waldorf education offers each individual teacher to determine the practices of their early childhood program can be misinterpreted to mean that "anything goes," according to their own personal preferences and style. Here too there is the danger that the developmental realities and needs of the children are not sufficiently taken into consideration.

Each of these one-sided approaches may be injurious to the development of the children. As Waldorf early childhood educators, we are constantly seeking a middle, universally human path between polarities. Rudolf Steiner's advice to the first Waldorf kindergarten teacher, Elizabeth Grunelius, in the early 1920s, could be paraphrased as follows: Observe the children. Actively meditate. Follow your intuitions. Work out of imitation.

Today we are challenged to engage in a constant process of renewal as Waldorf early childhood educators, actively observing today's children in our care, carrying them in our meditations, and seeking to work consciously and artistically to create the experiences that will serve their development. Our devotion to this task awakens us to the importance of self-education and transformation in the context of community. Our ongoing study of child and human development, our own artistic and meditative practices, and our work with anthroposophy, independently and together with others, become essential elements for the practice of Waldorf early childhood education. Here we can come to experience that we are not alone on this journey; we are supported through our encounters with one other and with spiritual beings offering support toward our continued development and toward the renewal of culture Waldorf education seeks to serve.

II. The Child Contemplation Form: A Potent Tool for Waldorf Schools in Challenging Times

Laurie Clark, in collaboration with the WECAN Early Childhood Research Group

Covid-19 has brought challenges to Waldorf communities on every level. Here in North America, schools are struggling to cope with major pedagogical, social, and financial questions. While solving everyday problems is a necessary priority, in order to move beyond merely reacting to these bigger challenges, we may need to remind ourselves to take time to listen and speak with one another. Sharing our stories helps us to realize that we are not alone and that we can find soul strength with one another.

We also have the potent pedagogical practice of *child contemplation*, also called *child study*, that teachers use to support a child going through a developmental challenge or who might benefit from additional attention. Sometimes a faculty will also undertake a *class contemplation*. Both of these processes involve observation, imagination, and meditation and help us deepen our understanding of a child or a class.

Could we also use this kind of process to help us penetrate the deeper issues and gestures that are arising in our schools out of the current situation or in any period of significant change? Those of us who have practiced child contemplation know how revealing and healing the process can be.

There is an urgency at this time for each school to contemplate the communal environment with an open and honest transparency. It is vitally important to acknowledge, seek to understand, and deeply commit to integrating diversity, equity, and inclusion (DEI) in our schools. This contemplation can provide a pathway to taking action and aligning our environment with the ethical roots of social justice. Bringing awareness to these issues within the school has the potential to be regenerative and transformative.

One school that went through a difficult transition two years ago initiated a version of this process, arising out of a sense that outside pressures had pulled the school away from its center, allowing it to become more and more Matter without Spirit. Some faculty members also carried the question of "What is the Being of the school?"[16] Their school contemplation process helped them rediscover and recommit to actively working with the spiritual impulses at the core of their work.

The following section offers one possible approach to a school contemplation process. It can be used as is or as a starting point for schools to develop their own processes.

School Contemplation Process

Open the session by reading a verse that is meaningful in your community.

I. The social mission of Waldorf education

- Recall the founding of the first Waldorf School and its social impulses.
- Read your school's mission, vision, and core values. Is there an alignment of the original vision and values with the mission of your school?

II. Our school's biography

- Share the inner and outer qualities of your place: geography, climate, and ecology; physical characteristics of the buildings and campus; organizational structures; the balance of long-term and newer teachers; the balance of tradition and innovation; the soul mood.

- Recall the history of your school from its inception to the present time, including who the founding members were, how the name was chosen, major milestones, accomplishments, and crises.

III. Awakening to community

- How does each individual, group, and the school as a whole stay aligned with the school's mission, vision, and values?

- How can we continue to stay awake to the spiritual being of the school?

- How can we invite our spiritual helpers to meet us in our endeavors?

IV. Reflections on initiatives for diversity, equity, and inclusion in our school

- Describe how the school is implementing DEI awareness and how it is coordinating plans in the faculty, administration, leadership structures, and parent community.

- How is DEI sustained and incorporated in the school's mission and policies (i.e., hiring, admissions)? Is there a diversity committee? Is there a safe place to share grievances?

- What is the mood and quality of the DEI work? What plans can be put into place to increase diversity and ensure a more equitable future for the school?

V. Reflections on our present circumstances

- What aspects of the school are healthy and thriving?
- In what areas are we currently facing challenges?
- Is there an archetypal image or story that characterizes the present situation?

VI. Steps towards healing and renewal

- What images are arising that can bring balance or healing to the situation?
- Are structural changes needed?
- How can we strengthen our relationships?
- How can we communicate and deal with conflict more creatively?

VII. Moving into the future with courage

Let us never forget that every step taken at the prompting of the spiritual world leads us into a situation where we have to look right and left and make a new decision. These decisions that are continually facing us have to be made with courage, with inner courage of life.
—RUDOLF STEINER, LECTURE 2,
THE CURATIVE EDUCATION COURSE

- What are our visions of the future?
- How can we support one another in our work together?

It would be ideal to be able to work through the steps of this process over the course of three days or three faculty meetings. Parts I and II could be completed in the first session, III and IV in the second session, and V and VI in the last session. This allows for questions to be worked with in the night and over time. Reviewing the results of the work together at a later date would also be fruitful.

Appendices

Coming to clear insights is a critical first step in meeting the need for change. Creating and implementing plans is a second step that requires different kinds of meetings and resources. Our inner attitude towards the children in our care makes a difference in their lives. In the same way, our teachers' and school leaders' attention to inner spiritual activity makes a difference in how practical solutions to meeting the challenges of our times unfold.

III. The Sevenfold Path—
An Outline for Child Contemplation
Laurie Clark

Calendar of the Soul Verse

To begin, read the verse matching the child's date of birth.

Part One—Picturing the Child

- Give a complete physical description—what stands out for you?
- Review the child's four foundational senses:
    - Touch: Over-sensitive sense of touch? Under-sensitive sense of touch? Comfortable with touch?
    - Movement: Describe how the child moves; demonstrate movements
    - Balance: Does the child fall often? Are they. cautious in movement? Fidgety? Do they have strong balance?
    - Life: How is the child's sense of well-being? Are they nervous? Restless? Calm? Overactive? Underactive?
- Describe the child's behaviors
    - Is the child able to imitate?
    - Does the child participate in activities in the class? Avoid certain activities?

- Describe the child's relationship to others
  - Children?
  - Adults?
- Describe the child's play:
  - Does the child play alone?
  - With other children?
  - Parallel play?
- Ability to transition from one activity to the next
- Speech: Volume, pitch, articulation, flow of breath
- What is the driving force that encouraged you to do this child study?

Part Two—Revelation of Soul Depths

- The gaze: Steiner pointed out that when we observe a child, we can experience something emanating from the child's gaze that reveals itself from out of the depth of their soul.
- Does the child's gaze reach out in social participation or is it withdrawn? Does it meet the gaze of others? Imitate the child's gaze. What is it expressing? What does it feel like?
- What is an image found in a fairytale, myth, or other story that mirrors the situation of the child? Is there an image out of nature that mirrors that child?

Part Three—Polarities

Information on the constitutional polarities can be found in *Understanding Deeper Development Needs: Holistic Approaches for Challenging Behaviors in Children* by Adam Blanning, MD (Great Barrington, MA: Lindisfarne Books, 2017).

BECOMING AND BELONGING

- Does the child live more in gravity or in levity?
- Are they active or passive?
- Introverted or extroverted?
- Wakeful or dreamy?
- Too much or too little?
- What other polarity or polarities stand out for you?

Part Four—Thresholds

- Describe the child's breathing:
  - Mouth open?
  - Even?
  - Shallow or deep?
  - Sighs?
  - Yawns?
- Waking and sleeping:
  - Deep sleeper?
  - Light sleeper?
  - Difficulty falling asleep?
  - Difficulty waking?
- Nutrition:
  - Allergies?
  - Food preferences?
  - Avoidances?
  - Digestion?
  - Chewing?
- Habits:

Appendices

- Thumb sucker?
- Nail biter?
- Chews clothes?

Mirror the child's being inside you. Feel into the child's being and describe what it feels like to be this child.

~

Review

This completes the first portion of the child contemplation. A short review of what has been discussed in these first steps is helpful in the next session before proceeding with parts five through seven.

~

Part Five—Entry into the World

- Describe the pregnancy:
    - Was it a surprise or planned?
    - Full term?
    - Any dreams the parents had of the child during pregnancy or before conception?
- Describe the delivery.
- What was the child like immediately after birth?
    - Awake?
    - Sleepy?
    - Alert?
    - Dreamy?
- How did parents find and decide on the child's name?
- Look up the meaning of the child's name.

BECOMING AND BELONGING

Create an artistic piece (poem, verse, story, drawing, felted picture, sculpture or painting) that represents and mirrors the child, encouraging them on their path in life.

Part Six—Footprints into Life

- Biography
- Developmental milestones
- Assessment information shared
- Child's drawings and paintings shared

Part Seven—Conclusions and Beginnings

- Share ideas and suggestions for the child.
- Express gratitude toward the child.
- Read the *Calendar of the Soul* verse again.
- Share a few silent moments at the end of the contemplation process.

Appendices

IV. Rudolf Steiner's Six Basic Exercises

These exercises are found in Rudolf Steiner's Esoteric Development, *Lecture 1 (GA 54), December 7, Berlin.*

To begin with, we must become masters over our thoughts and, particularly, our train of thought. This is called *control of thoughts*. Just think how thoughts whirl about in the soul of man, how they flit about like will-o'-the-wisps. Here one impression arises, there another, and each one changes one's thoughts. It is not true that we govern our thoughts; rather our thoughts govern us totally. We must advance to the ability of steeping ourselves in one specific thought at a certain time of the day and not allow any other thought to enter and disturb our soul. In this way we ourselves hold the reins of thought life for a time.

The second quality is to find a similar relationship to our actions, that is, to exercise *control over our actions*. Here it is necessary to undertake actions, at least occasionally, which are not initiated by anything external. That which is initiated by our station in life, our profession, or our situation does not lead us more deeply into higher life. Higher life depends on personal matters, such as resolving to do something springing totally from one's own initiative even if it is an absolutely insignificant matter. All other actions contribute nothing to the higher life.

The third quality to be striven for is *even-temperedness*. People fluctuate back and forth between joy and sorrow. One moment they are beside themselves with joy, the next they are unbearably sad. Thus, people allow themselves to be rocked on the waves of life, on joy or sorrow. But they must reach equanimity and steadiness. Neither the greatest sorrow nor the greatest joy must unsettle their composure. They must become steadfast and even-tempered.

Fourth is the *understanding for every being*. Nothing expresses more beautifully what it means to understand every being than the legend, which is handed down to us, not by the Gospel, but by a Persian story. Jesus was walking across a field with his disciples, and on the way, they found a decaying dog. The animal looked horrible. Jesus stopped and cast an admiring look upon it, saying, "What beautiful teeth the animal has!" Jesus found within the ugly the one beautiful aspect. Strive at all times to approach what is wonderful in every object of outer reality, and you will see that everything contains an aspect that can be affirmed. Do as Christ did when he admired the beautiful teeth on the dead dog. This course will lead you to the great ability to tolerate, and to an understanding of everything and of every being.

The fifth quality is *complete openness* towards everything new that meets us. Most people judge new things which meet them by the old which they already know. If anyone comes to tell them something new, they immediately respond with an opposing opinion. But we must not confront a new communication immediately with our own opinion. We must rather be on the alert for possibilities of learning something new. And learn we can, even from a small child. Even if one were the wisest person, one must be willing to hold back one's own judgment, and to listen to others. We must develop this ability to listen, for it will enable us to meet matters with the greatest possible openness. In occultism, this is called faith. It is the power not to weaken through opposition the impression made by the new.

The sixth quality is that which everyone receives once he has developed the first five. It is *inner harmony*. The person who has the other qualities also has inner harmony. In addition, it is necessary for a person seeking occult development to develop his feeling for freedom to the highest degree. That feeling for freedom enables him to seek within himself the center of his own being, to stand on his own two feet, so that he will not have to ask everyone what he should do and so that he can stand upright and act freely. This also is a quality which one needs to acquire.

If man has developed these qualities within himself, then he stands above all the dangers arising from the division within his nature. Then the properties of his lower nature can no longer affect him; he can no longer stray from the path. Therefore, these qualities must be formed with the greatest precision. Then comes the occult life, whose expression depends on a steady rhythm being carried into life.

V. The Artistic Meeting: Creating Space for Spirit
Holly Koteen-Soulé

When Rudolf Steiner brought together the individuals who would become the teachers of the first Waldorf school, he asked them to work in a new way, not only with the children, but also with one another. He asked them to work together in such as way as to invite the interest and guidance of spiritual beings into their endeavor.

The challenge of creating and maintaining a connection with the spiritual world, as difficult as it was then, may be even more intense in the present time. Materialism has grown considerably stronger in the twenty-first century, and with it has come an increasing need to bring a balancing, healing, and renewing element to daily life.

The Waldorf classroom is a place where this renewing spiritual element can be found. It arises from the children themselves and from how we work with them. It can also be found in the meeting life of the school, in how the teachers and other adults work together. There are many resources available today on conducting effective meetings in the workplace. This article will focus on how we can create a space for spirit in meetings, and how this endeavor can support us in our individual development, in our encounters with colleagues, and in strengthening our groups and communities.

Meetings as artistic activity will be a second focus. Understanding meetings as an art form and using an artistic approach in planning and carrying out a meeting will more likely allow participants to be refreshed and inspired at the meeting's conclusion. While including an artistic activity in the agenda can be helpful, it is more critical that the meeting itself be artistic and display the wholeness, drama, and dynamics of any other artistic creation. Artistic activity can often be a doorway to the recognition of spiritual archetypes and the building of spiritual understanding. A meeting that is conducted as a form of art greatly enhances this possibility for the participants.

Meetings as Spiritual Practice

Waking Up in the Other

Near the end of his life, after the burning of the first Goetheanum and during a period of upheaval within the Anthroposophical Society, Rudolf Steiner began to speak urgently about the need to build communities based on a shared spiritual purpose that extends beyond our cultural or hereditary ties. He described physical waking as a response to the stimuli of the natural world in our surroundings. Our waking up at a higher level happens when we encounter the soul-spirit of other human beings. He went so far as to say:

> We are also unable to understand the spiritual world, no matter how many beautiful ideas we may have garnered from anthroposophy or how much we may have grasped theoretically about such matters as etheric and astral bodies. We begin to develop an understanding for the spiritual world only when we wake up in the encounter with the soul-spiritual in our fellowmen.[17]

On other occasions, Steiner also spoke about a need in our age (the fifth post-Atlantean epoch) that can only be fulfilled in groups. He referred specifically to the spirit of fellowship hovering above us in the realm of the higher hierarchies, which needs to be consciously cultivated so that it can flow into human souls in the future. These statements constitute a strong call for us to create opportunities for more, rather than fewer, encounters with our colleagues, despite the inevitable challenges with which we are all familiar.

The Reverse Ritual

In considering meetings as spiritual practice, it may be helpful to recall our understanding from anthroposophy that at a certain point in the course of the evolution of the cosmos and humanity, the higher creative beings drew back from the sphere of the earth. This withdrawal was necessary in order for human beings to develop in freedom. As a result, the physical earth is in the process of dying. The human being, having been given freedom and the possibility of spiritual consciousness, has become an increasingly decisive factor in the future of the earth.

One of our tasks is to help re-enliven the earth. We do that with the substance of our human thinking—not our ordinary thoughts and reflections, but spiritual thoughts arising from creative "Imaginations," "Inspirations," and "Intuitions." These creative thoughts represented for Steiner a new spiritual form of communion for humanity. He gave many indications for how both individuals and groups could work with creative, enlivening thoughts for their own benefit and for humanity as a whole.

It was Steiner's deep conviction that the appropriate form for community-building in our time is what he called the reverse ritual. He distinguished this ritual from a traditional religious ritual in which a mediator is charged with drawing the spiritual hierarchies down to a particular place. "The anthroposophical community seeks to lift up the human souls into supersensible worlds so that they may enter into the company of angels."[18]

> We must do more than talk about spiritual beings; we must look for opportunities nearest at hand to enter their company. The work of an anthroposophical group does not consist in a number of people merely discussing anthroposophical ideas. Its members should feel so linked with one another that human soul wakes up in the encounter with human soul and all are lifted up into the spiritual world, into the company of spiritual beings, though it need not be

a question of beholding them. We do not have to see them to have this experience.[19]

The "College Imagination" or the "Teacher's Imagination" that Steiner gave to the first group of teachers is an example of such a reverse ritual, in which a group working with a common meditative picture creates the possibility of connecting with specific spiritual beings and bringing back creative impulses for their earthly work.[20]

If Waldorf teachers wish to work with these ideas and with the example of the "Teacher's Imagination," how can we form and conduct faculty and college meetings in this light? How can our meeting life be spiritually sustaining for individuals and build a vital sense of community in our schools?

Space for Spirit

We know what it feels like to have participated in a successful meeting. We are enlivened at the meeting's end. We also know that what occurred could not have been achieved by any individual member of the group. These are indicators of spirit presence. It is possible to learn how to create such meetings—meetings that lift us out of our ordinary awareness and allow us the possibility of working more consciously with the spiritual world. We can create more space for spirit in our meeting life in the following ways.

(1) *Imbue the meeting place with a sense of conscious care.* It is often the case that certain individuals have a natural feeling for the need to prepare the room where a meeting will occur. When we prepare a space with care we are working with the elementals, spiritual beings which, according to Rudolf Steiner, are detachments from the higher hierarchies, sacrificing themselves for the creation of the material world. They have a great deal to do with the physical setting, and also with our individual physical well-being, our thinking, feeling, and willing, and our communication.

In my own experience, how the room is prepared can have as significant an effect on a meeting as it does on what happens in our classrooms when we make sure that they are clean, orderly, and beautiful. Imagine how the arrangement of the furniture could enhance the quality of the group's interaction. Consider the effect of having as a centerpiece a seasonal bouquet gathered by a member of the group, rather than one that was purchased at the florist shop. It is especially helpful if all members of a faculty take a turn at preparing the setting, so that more members of the group carry the importance of this aspect of the meeting.

(2) *Create a threshold mood.* Meetings that begin with a moment of silence and a mood of reverence allow participants to be aware of stepping across a kind of threshold, out of our everyday consciousness into a heightened sense of presence. An explicit acknowledgment of our spiritual helpers, the spirit of the school, and those persons who have been connected to our institution and are now in the spiritual world, can also shift the group's awareness. A conscious effort to begin on time helps create the sense of going through a doorway together. A verse can also represent a threshold and when brought in the right mood, offer a kind of protective sheath for whatever may happen in the meeting.

(3) *Re-establish the sense of the group.* This activity has two parts. The first is the recognition of individuals and the second is an affirmation of the purpose of the group. A key to the first part is the interest that we take in one another. Listening to colleagues share something out of their lives or an aspect of their work with students can wake us up to one another in a potent way. The sharing can be brief and, in the case of a large faculty, may involve only a portion of the group each week. Sharing can also be connected to the season; for example, at Michaelmas, the focus could be, "What in your life is requiring a fresh burst of courage and will?"

This part of the meeting can deepen our understanding of our colleagues and build the level of trust that we need to work together on spiritual matters. Movement or artistic activity can also serve to strengthen the group's capacity to work together on issues that require sensitivity to one another. At this stage of the meeting the "I" of each individual is acknowledged as he or she steps into the work with the group, or the "We."

The second part of establishing the sense of the group is an affirmation of the group's purpose or task. A verse or reading can be helpful, but must be relevant and alive for the group. For some groups, it may be important to choose a new opening for each year or to work with festival themes in order to strengthen the sense of community and purpose at this stage of the meeting. For other groups, choosing to work consciously with the same verse for many years may actually bring them to an ever-deepening understanding of its meaning and effect. While study is often used to bring a group to a common focus, this is successful only if everyone is actively engaged.

(4) *Practice conscious listening and speaking.* We know that listening perceptively to another person requires letting go of our sympathies and antipathies and our own preconceived ideas; in fact, we must momentarily let go of our own I to experience the "I" of the other as they speak. Marjorie Spock wrote most poetically about the effects of perceptive listening.

> First, there is what it does to the soul of the listener. A miracle of self-overcoming takes place within him whenever he really lends an ear to others. If he is to understand the person speaking, he must draw his attention from his own concerns and make a present of it to a listener; he clears his inner scene like one who for a time gives up his home for others' use while himself remaining only in the role of servant. Listeners quite literally entertain a speaker's thought. "Not I, but the Christ in me" is made real in every such act of genuine listening.
>
> Second, there is what happens to the speaker when he is fortunate to be listened to perceptively. Another kind of miracle takes place in him, perhaps best described as a springtime burgeoning. Before his idea was expressed to a listener, it lived in his soul as potential only; it resembles a seed force lying fallow in the winter earth. To be

> listened to with real interest acts upon this seed like sun and warmth and rain and other cosmic elements that provide growth-impetus; the soul ground in which the idea is embedded comes magically alive. Under such benign influence, thoughts grow full cycle and fulfill their promise. Moreover they confer fertility upon the ground through the simple fact of having lived there. Further ideas will be the more readily received into such a soil and spring more vigorously for its life-attunement. And the soul that harbors them begins to be the creative force in evolution for which it was intended by the gods.[21]

Brief spaces of silence can also allow thoughts and insights to ripen and fall into the conversation. Can we provide for the seed thoughts of our colleagues, out of our own souls, what the sun and rain provide for the sprouting plant? It is a rare group that does not need to recommit regularly to practicing this kind of listening and speaking.

(5) *Work with imaginative pictures over time.* Imagination is a language that can bear fruit in the spiritual world. Translating the group's questions and issues into stories and pictures can enhance the group's meditative work during the meeting or individual work during the course of the week. Look for an archetype, myth or fairy tale that can reveal new aspects of the matter under consideration. Taking time over two or three meetings to explore major questions invites the possibility of richer insights to come forth. Colleagues will want to hold back from building support for one or another course of action and to be open to new information as it emerges during this phase. Having worked successfully with imaginative pictures in the child study process can help colleagues trust their use in other situations as well.

(6) *Share responsibility.* Individuals who are able to carry the consciousness for a group have certain capacities that are usually recognized by the other members of the group. Not everyone has these in the same measure, but it is important to recognize talents among colleagues and give one another opportunities and support to develop latent capacities.

Different individuals can lead various parts of a meeting. A group of two or three people can plan the agenda. Incorporate means of regular feedback and review for those taking responsibility in the yearly schedule.

It is clear that a group is healthiest when individuals are continuing to grow and develop. Even the most competent facilitator needs to step back or work with a new colleague in order to gain fresh perspective. Rotating leadership and having several individuals to carry one or another aspect of the meeting facilitation makes it more likely that all members will feel involved. All members are responsible to bring to the group the results of their individual meditative life. Spiritual leadership requires learning how to create the conditions for meaningful conversations and then helping the group follow up on what arises out of those conversations.

(7) *Let the meeting breathe.* In our work in the classroom we need to prepare carefully and also be ready to respond to what comes from our students. A meeting that has a compelling wholeness and feeling of flow is probably the result of a well-crafted agenda along with some adjustments made during the meeting to an emerging sense of clarity and direction. Having prior agreements about how to deal with new information or agenda changes is helpful. A rhythmic relation to time in a meeting creates more of an opening for spiritual insights than either an overstuffed agenda or a formless one.

There are a number of simple possibilities for making a meeting more rhythmic. For example, honor the times on the agenda, but not so rigidly that people feel cut off or topics are truncated. Vary the conversation from full-group sharing to small-group work and individual reports. Create a balance between pedagogical and other topics, looking back and looking ahead, exploring new questions and making decisions. When the group is not moving physically, make sure there is plenty of inner movement. Remember to invite the spirit of Play and the spirit of Humor into the meeting.

(8) *Expect to be surprised.* There is nothing more uninviting than a completely predictable meeting. On the other hand, a meeting in which the group is pulled this way and that by personal agendas is equally frustrating. We must stay awake to the influences of Ahriman (too much form) and Lucifer (too much impulse) as they work in individuals and in our groups.

In order to stay the course in the creative spiritual stream, we need to ask real questions; practice positivity and open-mindedness; be comfortable with not knowing; and expect answers and solutions to come from unexpected places.

(9) *Review.* During meeting review, we give ourselves feedback on what went well and what could have been better, so that we can improve our work together. Review serves another important purpose as well. Just as our nightly review is a conversation starter for the work with our own angel during sleep, our meeting review serves as a seed for the continuing conversation with the spiritual world between meetings.

Running late in a meeting is sometimes the reason that groups neglect review, but review can often capture essential aspects of a meeting in a brief and economical way. In this regard, poetry is more useful than prose. Brief characterizations, even one-word or one-image offerings, can illuminate hidden gems. Hearing individual voices during the review can be a supportive bookend to the work, like the personal sharing at the beginning of a meeting.

Review is not a rehashing of any part of the meeting. It should bring to light aspects of content, processes, and interactions that can benefit from greater awareness on the part of individuals and the group. A perceptive facilitator will vary the means of review and offer questions to elicit information that might not otherwise be brought to light. "Where did we experience gratitude in the meeting?" "Were there any moments of unresolved tension?" "What did we do that might be of interest to our spiritual helpers?" Review in the form of an earnest question is the best kind of invitation to spirit beings.

(10) *Prepare and follow up.* If we recognize our meetings as a kind of ritual, then the preparation and the follow-up are as important as the meeting itself. Preparation requires more than a quick glance at a copy of the agenda. When individuals come to a meeting having thought about the issues and their colleagues the night before, the spiritual ground has already been tilled.

How we carry the questions as well as the tasks from one meeting to the next can make a difference in whether the seeds sowed will sprout healthily in the coming weeks. How each individual carries the group in between meetings will also make a difference. Working rhythmically with time has both a physical and a spiritual aspect. When we consciously release ideas that have arisen in the group into the spiritual world, it is possible that they will return in a more complete or archetypal form.

These are some of the realities that we may wish to take into consideration as we build a vessel for the spiritual aspect of our work, just as we pay attention to earthly realities in constructing a physical home for our schools.

Meetings as Art

The Artistic Process

The arts, according to Rudolf Steiner, were experienced in earlier civilizations as more integral to life than is the case today. Artistic creativity, he said, was experienced as a transcendent spiritual activity, flowing out of the "spirit-attuned state" in which the human being lived in those times. Only since the rise of materialism has the status of art changed from necessity to luxury.

Rudolf Steiner also observed that in our era a longing for the arts comes out of the recognition of the limits of abstract thinking. Ideas alone are not able to illuminate the world in its full richness; they can only point the way to a deeper reality. Artistic feeling, Steiner said, arises when we sense the presence of something mysterious, such as certain secrets of nature, which can only be revealed through our feeling. Knowing is a matter for the heart as well as the head. To discover a whole, living reality, we need to create, to practice art. He saw the fructification of the arts in our time as an important task for anthroposophy, and he took up various artistic projects himself during the latter part of his life.

The present-day artist engaged in the creative process moves back and forth between sense perceptions and intuitive visions—awake, but in a somewhat dreamlike feeling state. Steiner described the subtle changes that occur in a person engaged in aesthetic activity (regardless of whether the person is creating or enjoying an artistic creation) such that the sense organs are re-enlivened and the bodily life processes are lifted to soul-like processes.

In artistic activity we use our heightened sense of feeling rather than our everyday sympathies and antipathies. The artist, consciously or unconsciously, approaches the threshold between the sensible and supersensible worlds and brings something back from the supersensible world into the world of the senses. The resulting creation is a specifically experienced reality lifted into a universal expression.

As Waldorf teachers we understand the importance of the arts and our own creativity in the work with our students. Can we also imagine applying a consciously artistic approach and a heightened sense of feeling to our work with our colleagues in our meetings?

Social Art

In the series of lectures *Art as Seen in the Light of Mystery Wisdom*, Steiner connected each of the arts with the various members of the human being. The laws of the physical body, he said, are expressed in architecture, the etheric in sculpture, the astral in painting, and the ego in music. The still developing spirit self he connected to poetry and the life spirit to eurythmy. The highest art, according to Steiner, is social art.

The first three arts—architecture, sculpture, and painting (including drawing)—are the spatial arts. These are derived out of formative processes and past evolutionary cycles. They are connected to sculptural forces working out of the past and, in the context of education, help children come into their bodily constitution.

In contrast, the time arts—music, speech and poetry, and eurythmy—are connected to impulses coming out of the future. As Waldorf teachers we work out of our higher bodies and what Steiner called our musical forces in order to guide our students properly into their present life. Social art also belongs to this group of time arts, but is younger, less tangible, and even less developed than eurythmy. How can we study and practice this least tangible of arts?

My own experience is that working in any of the other arts can serve as a basic "instruction manual" for social art. Being grounded in an artistic practice makes it easier to apply the principles of creative activity to any aspect of life, including social situations.

As an early childhood teacher, when I had a particularly satisfying day in the kindergarten, I felt as if the children and I had spent the whole morning moving to an exquisite piece of music. When I was responsible for meetings, I began to plan agendas as if I were composing or painting and, during the meeting, I tried to pay attention to compositional elements like repetition, variation, contrast, harmony, balance, focus, surprise, and reprise.

In addition to the writings of Rudolf Steiner, we can also learn about social art in certain traditional texts where the renewing or healing spiritual element is represented symbolically: the "water of life" from the world of fairy tales, the Grail in the legend of Parsifal, the philosopher's stone of the alchemists, and conversation in Goethe's tale, "The Green Snake and the Beautiful Lily."

In North America we owe a great debt to Marjorie Spock, who brought Steiner's concern for community-building to us. She translated Steiner's *Awakening to Community* lectures into English and wrote two little pamphlets, *Group Moral Artistry*, that are a continuing inspiration for many people. Goethean conversation was the term she used to characterize the process by which a group could invite truth into their midst like a guest. She began with Goethe's framing of conversation as the art of arts and described Goethean conversation as a form of the reverse ritual and an appropriate means of practicing social artistry.

Artistic Meetings

Our artistic sensibilities and an artistic approach to our work in a meeting can enhance the possibility of lifting ourselves into the company of angels, if only briefly. Meetings can be artistic in a number of ways.

A meeting can be artistic because we consciously include an artistic activity in the agenda and allow what flows out of that activity to enhance the rest of our work together. It can also be artistic in the way we use imaginative pictures to enrich our conversations or moments of silence to invite creative inspirations. When the meeting itself is seen as an artistic process, the facilitator and the group will be more likely to strive for a palpable sense of aliveness and wholeness. Finally, if we take our work in the social arts seriously, whatever we are able to achieve in the special situation of our meetings has the potential to strengthen our relationships overall and may even have a healing effect on other relationships in the community.

Conscious Conversation—An Invitation

We swim in a sea of spirit. Our matter-bound everyday consciousness, however, easily forgets the reality of spirit living in and everywhere around us. In this age of Michael especially, we have to wake up in those places where we are sleepily swept along with the materialistic tides of existence. It is not easy to push aside pressing everyday concerns again and again to make space for encounters with spirit in one another and with spirit beings on the other side of the threshold.

As Waldorf teachers, this is a task that we have taken on, not only for the sake of our students, but also because the conversation with the spirit is the source of our own strength, inspiration, and creativity. In our meeting life and through an artistic practice of conscious conversation, we have an incredible opportunity to enter as a group into the realm of spirit-sensing. Our own work as individuals, as well as the whole Waldorf movement, needs this renewing spiritual force as it continues to grow and proliferate throughout the world.

REFERENCES AND ADDITIONAL READING

Howard, Michael. *Art as Spiritual Activity: Rudolf Steiner's Contribution to the Visual Arts*. Great Barrington, MA: Anthroposophic Press, 1998.

Spock, Marjorie. *Group Moral Artistry*. Volume 1, *Reflections on Community Building*. Spring Valley, NY: St George Publications, 1983.

——. *Group Moral Artistry*. Volume 2, *Goethean Conversation*. Spring Valley, NY: St George Publications, 1983.

Steiner, Rudolf. *Art as Seen in the Light of Mystery Wisdom*. Eight lectures held in Dornach from December 28, 1914, to January 4, 1915. London: Rudolf Steiner Press, 1984.

——. *The Arts and their Mission*. Hudson, NY: Anthroposophic Press, 1964.

——. *Awakening to Community*. Ten lectures given in Stuttgart and Dornacht, January 23–March 4, 1923. Spring Valley, NY: Anthroposophic Press, 1974.

——. *The Foundations of Human Experience*. Hudson, NY: Anthroposophic Press, 1996.

Steiner, Rudolf, and Friedrich Benesch. *Reverse Ritual: Spiritual Knowledge Is True Communion*. Great Barrington, MA: Anthroposophic Press, 2001.

Van den Brink, Margarete. *More Precious Than Light: How Dialogue Can Transform Relationships and Build Community*. Stroud, England: Hawthorn Press, 1996.

Zimmermann, Heinz. *Speaking, Listening, Understanding: The Art of Creating Conscious Conversation*. Translated by James H. Hindes. Hudson, NY: Anthroposophic Press, 1996.

ENDNOTES TO THE APPENDICES

1 Rudolf Steiner, *The Child's Changing Consciousness* (Hudson, NY: Anthroposophic Press, 1996), 141.

2 Rudolf Steiner, *The Education of the Child and Early Lectures on Education* (Hudson, NY: Anthroposophic Press, 1996), 22.

3 *Education of the Child*, 18.

4 Rudolf Steiner, "A Modern Art of Education," lecture of August 10, 1923, in *On the Play of the Child: Indications by Rudolf Steiner for Working with Young Children*, translated by Jan-Kees Saltet (Spring Valley, NY: Waldorf Early Childhood Association of North America, 2012), 30.

5 *Child's Changing Consciousness*, 72.

6 *Education of the Child*, 19.

7 Rudolf Steiner, *Self-Education in the Light of Anthroposophy* (Spring Valley, NY: Mercury Press, 1995).

8   Rudolf Steiner, "Education in the Face of the Present-Day Situation," a lecture dated June 10, 1920, GA 335, in *On the Play of the Child,* 32.

9   Steiner, "A Modern Art of Education," in *On the Play of the Child,* 31.

10 *Child's Changing Consciousness,* 125–26.

11 Ibid., 127.

12 *Education of the Child,* 22.

13 Rudolf Steiner, *The Kingdom of Childhood* (Hudson, NY: 1995), 19.

14 Rudolf Steiner, *The Essentials of Education* (Hudson, NY: SteinerBooks/Anthroposophic Press, 2019), 14.

15 Rudolf Steiner, "Education in the Face of the Present-Day World Situation," in *On the Play of the Child,* 33.

16 Johannes Tautz Wilton discusses the "Being of the School" *in The Meditative Life of the Teacher: Three Lectures* (NH: Pedagogical Section Council of North America, 1986. The lectures took place on June 18–20, 1986. Tautz describes how, just two days after the first Waldorf school's opening, the founding teachers gathered to take on the task of forming a faculty. They wanted to form a faculty that was aware of itself as a responsible community, working in cooperation with all of its members. In this way, the community could become capable of inviting the being of the school into its presence, and could become an organ for this being. It was essential for this faculty to commit to a regular, rhythmic relationship to this spiritual experience through a practice of soul exercises. Experience confirms that a spiritual practice by the community members of the school invokes the "Being of the school" and helps the essence of the school to manifest. It also works constructively into the healthy social life of the community.

17 Rudolf Steiner, *Awakening to Community,* 97.

18 Ibid, 157.

19 Ibid.

20 For a description of the Imagination, see *The Foundations of Human Experience,* 45-48.

21 Marjorie Spock, *Reflections on Community Building* (*Group Moral Artistry* vol. 1), 18.